Dedication

To: Anna Jane Hildebolt

and

To all the mothers in the world who loved their babies
and allowed them to grow up to be cowboys and cowgirls,
just as long as they were professionals!

Acknowledgments

The idea for this book evolved from discussions with Rod Dickens as we were planning the outlines for my monthly president's messages that would be published in the PLANET news magazine. As president of the Professional Landcare Network (PLANET), a green industry trade association, I was responsible for 12 monthly letters to the membership, and Rod Dickens helped to make sure that everything that went into print was well organized and met the publishing standards of the magazine. As I shared my vision of using professionalism as the continuity theme for the letters, we quickly realized that there was far too much material to cover in 12 brief messages. We mutually came up with the idea that maybe I had the makings for a book on the subject.

The origins of the material that is captured in this book have deep roots, and specifically, I have to credit a former RJR colleague Harold Threatt for help in the origination of the four-legged stool concept to illustrate the basic tenets of professionalism. I first used this approach in a training session for the production and administration staff of Nature's Select Premium Turf Services, Inc. This turned out to be an effective teaching/training tool that encouraged good interactions among the trainees and the instructors; so I used this model to develop the structure for this book.

As part of the book, Rod Dickens and I decided that I should conduct interviews with top professionals. This would not only increase the knowledge base of the book but would allow me to incorporate real-life stories into the context of professional characteristics.

Special thanks go to family members: my son Bill, my wife Sandi, and my uncle Charles for their patient reading and editorial skills, and again to Harold Threatt and Rod Dickens for their encouragement, insights, and many rewrites.

The Professional Entrepreneur

The PROFESSIONAL ENTREPRENEUR

When Cowboys Grow Up

WILLIAM HILDEBOLT

The Professional Entrepreneur

Foreword

Before you begin to read this book, it is important to know that it is divided into two distinct sections. The first section consists of five chapters that are an overview of professionalism, entrepreneurialism, and what I consider to be the defining characteristics of what it takes in today's high-paced, competitive, and diversified business world to become a professional and a successful entrepreneur. The second section of the book contains the interviews that I conducted with 12 people who have achieved the rare status of a professional entrepreneur in the green industry. These people have mastered the skills of their profession and applied these talents to become successful entrepreneurs. The interviews are in alphabetical order. The people interviewed were chosen because each had a unique journey in becoming a professional and achieving entrepreneurial success. In a number of instances, to support and enhance points that I make in the first section of the book and to maintain continuity throughout the book, I copied verbatim from the interviews in the second section of the book. It does not matter which section of the book is read first, and each interview in the second section is intended to be a freestanding profile that is independent of the other interviews. In writing the book, my intent was that it would make no difference which section of the book was read first nor would it make a difference if a reader were to skip back and forth between the interviews and first section of the book. Reading the book in such a fashion mimics how many professional entrepreneurs face new challenges - that is, they often do not follow standard procedures but instead are creative in how they do things.

While reading the book, you may recognize a chicken-and-egg causality dilemma and ask yourself, "What does one become first: a professional or an entrepreneur?" When I wrote the book's outline, I thought (based mostly on my own experiences) that becoming a professional comes first. As I conducted more and more interviews, I developed a neutral position, and now that I have written this book, I think that in many instances the main driving forces are desires to become entrepreneurs. Motivated by dreams of being their own bosses and controlling their destinies, some people become successful entrepreneurs, and some of these entrepreneurs subsequently develop professional characteristics. In retrospect, I think that the driving forces for me were twofold - my mother's encouragement to become a professional and the role models of my two entrepreneurial grandfathers. As you peruse each chapter and the interviews, determinc what motivated you to achieve your current career status; this may help you determine where you have been and where you are going. I return the to the chicken-and-egg causality dilemma at the end of the book.

Table of Contents

Author 1955

PROLOGUE

....

"Mamas, don't let your babies grow up to be cowboys." —Willie Nelson

When growing up in rural Ohio, all I ever wanted to be was a cowboy. School was difficult for me. I disliked being in class and spent most of the time day dreaming about being outdoors or inventing something. In my mind, being a cowboy would be more fun. Unfortunately or fortunately, as the case turned out to be, my schoolteacher mother Anna Jane had other plans for me. She impressed on me that being a cowboy was not an option, that I could become a professional in spite of my not liking school.

I credit her with giving me the inspiration to work hard toward becoming a professional. This book is a story of my thoughts and observations about how almost anyone who works hard can become a professional, despite the obstacles.

William Morton Hildebolt

CHAPTER I

Introduction to Professionalism

As you turn the pages in this book, please do not confuse the words with those of an expert in the field - someone who has devoted his or her life to researching and studying the subject of professionalism. This is not to imply that I am a novice on the subject - I have spent eight years as a farmer, three years as a teaching associate at a major university, 25 years as a corporate executive, 16 years as an entrepreneur, attended literally hundreds of conferences, studied numerous books on the subject, and more importantly have tried to live and work in a professional manner.

This book is based primarily on my personal experiences and those of industry professionals whom I have interviewed. I see myself as more of an observer than a scholar, and I do not consider myself to be a role model for professionalism. Some of the material (my observations and experiences) is original; some is borrowed; and some may be presented without appropriate acknowledgement of the source - if the latter occurs, it is not done so intentionally.

While writing this book, I became increasingly aware that it is not easy to define professionalism. Every field in every industry has different criteria and professional standards. The medical field requires doctors to go through years of rigorous training, internships, residencies, fellowships, and recurring certifications. At the other extreme are professional wrestlers who, in reality, set their own standards and rules - virtually accountable to no one other than their viewers and concomitant television ratings.

In this book, I discuss professionalism in the broadest sense of the word. This is not a textbook on the subject. If readers are interested in more scholarly interpretations of professionalism, good references are the *Harvard Business Review* and the works of authors such as Peter Drucker. The Internet is also a good source of information on professionalism.

I consider the value of this book to be that it is based on reality, grounded by years of personal experience - those of the professionals I have interviewed and mine. Although the book covers a lot of territory in relatively few pages, it is my hope that readers from many different industries will glean bits of knowledge that will be of lasting value to their lives and their professional careers.

Professionalism has evolved over the years. During Newton's time, doctors were not viewed in high esteem; instead, teachers and ministers held more of a professional status in their communities. In the mid-20th Century, doctors, lawyers, ministers, professors, and scientists were members of an elite club of professionals. By the end of the century, the explosion of the information age allowed more disciplines to join the professional ranks. Information technology professionals, accounting professionals, and social science professionals formed a larger elite club. The professional designation was no longer the exclusive domain of those with liberal arts educations; depending on the field, professionals were those with both advanced levels of education and hands-on, vocational training.

The green industry has been talking about "being more professional" for several decades. The thought is if the level of professionalism within the industry can be raised, its image, its ability to recruit new employees, and its pricing for services will also increase, allowing green entrepreneurs to become co-equals with other industry professionals. This is, however, easier said than done because being a professional requires more than wearing a uniform, driving a clean truck, and using the word "professional" when communicating with customers. As defined in Webster's, a professional is, "a person who, by education, training, and experience, performs work, analyzes and solves problems, makes decisions, and promotes ethics associated with a particular field."

In other words, being a professional encompasses several disciplines. I like to use the three-legged stool analogy when discussing the topic. The stool, in this case being a professional, is only as stable as its legs. If one leg is weak or fails, the stool collapses. If an individual lacks all the required attributes of being a professional, he or she, too, falls short of being a professional.

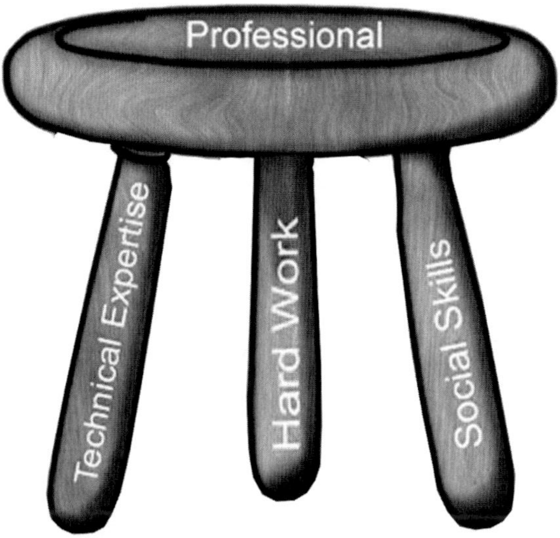

"What are these 'professional' legs, one may ask?" Simply put, being a professional requires having technical expertise in a chosen field, working hard to achieve goals, and having the social skills to successfully interact with customers, suppliers, and associates. As I discovered growing up on a farm, three legs are good, but four provide an even better foundation - a more stable stool. The fourth leg to being a professional is personal character, which, if lacking, undercuts any attempt to be a professional. All the technical expertise, hard work, and social skills in the world do not make up for flawed character traits - those that are evidenced by not being open, honest, sincere, trustworthy, and straightforward when dealing with people.

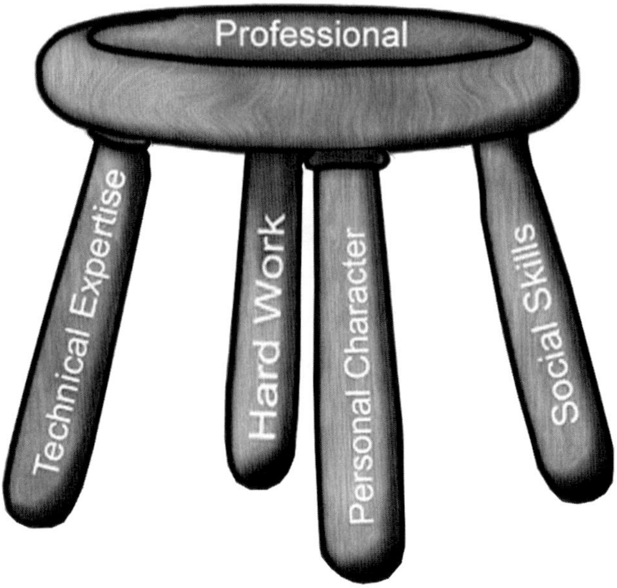

No wonder it can take an industry so long to develop a professional reputation. One does not become a professional overnight; it requires practice, forethought, guiding examples, and perseverance. It also requires having the wherewithal to keep the legs in balance. Granted, you cannot be too honest or forthright, but you can work too hard, spend an inordinate amount of time and money training, and go a bit overboard socializing.

Professionals learn to maintain a balance at work and to balance work with free time. Having a healthy balance at work and at home is critical to being healthy and living a long, rewarding life. Without this important balance (and your health), being a professional offers little reward.

Entrepreneurship

"It's flaps down, full throttle all the way"

When engaged in a new start up, an entrepreneur has to be totally committed. Years ago, when I was taking flying lessons, one of the first things my flight instructor told me was that during take-off, I had to put the flaps down and give the airplane full power. It was flaps down, full throttle all the way; there would be no second chance. It was either being totally committed to getting off the ground or risking crashing and burning.

Entrepreneurs have similar decisions to make – either being totally committed with their new ventures or risk crashing and burning. When Cortez invaded Mexico, the first move he made was to burn his ships. There was no turning back, he told his invading army. There would be no reserves, no knights on white horses to rescue them. Success meant that they would have to be completely committed to victory. Alexander the Great never retreated; he was always attacking and on the offense. In his mind, once the course was set, there was no second-guessing, no turning back. Successful entrepreneurs are also committed to their goals and avoid retreating in the face of hardships.

Propreneur

In the process of writing this book, several things became apparent to me that were not obvious before I began. My original plan was to focus on professionalism with emphasis on technical and social skills and one's character, but, as I interviewed top professionals, I detected underlying patterns that were both surprising and simple. All of the professionals started their careers at young ages by working odd jobs and in some cases by starting their own businesses. They set goals and worked hard to achieve their dreams. They were persistent and were not easily dissuaded when setbacks or adversities occurred. An additional underlying pattern was that the professionals were all entrepreneurs at heart. They not only had the characteristics of professionals but also had the overriding drive of entrepreneurs who want to control their own destinies, be their own bosses, and be in positions to make differences. To me, the individuals who achieve the rarefied rank of being top business or educational leaders and professionals are professional entrepreneurs that I like to call *propreneurs.*

CHAPTER II

Hard Work

"If it isn't hard, it isn't worth a damn!" - Woody Hayes

In physical terms, hard work is defined as an expenditure of energy. Climbing stairs is hard work, as is running. Running faster requires working harder. Letting one's mind wander, while one stands still or sits behind a desk, is not hard physical work. Based upon my experience, the higher one is on the corporate or administrative ladder, the less physical work one does. If you happen to have a "C" as part of your job title, you are probably up in arms by now but stay with me for a while.

Chief executive officers (CEOs), chief operating officers (COOs), and chief financial officers (CFOs) do mental work, put in long hours, and make tough decisions, but they do not do hard physical work. The physical work is being done by people on factory floors, by those serving customers in the field, and by back-office functionaries or salespeople who actually bring in the revenue. When you are at the top, you dictate your memos, and someone else schedules your meetings, answers your calls (maybe even dials the telephone for you), and organizes your travel. Someone in finance prepares your budget. You might approve it, but someone else pounded the numbers into the spreadsheet, just as someone else did the legwork to come up with the content. Meanwhile, external ad agencies craft your marketing message and the ads to communicate it. Outside counsel performs your legal and regulatory tasks. Consultants are called on to take on difficult reorganizing and downsizing decisions, and executive recruiters do your recruiting. Get the picture? If you operate in the upper reaches of the corporate world, you may be the ringmaster, but you are not doing the really hard physical work.

So, are the C-level executives useless? Of course not. C-level executives should manage and lead, not do. There is a difference and if you are a C-level executive who is doing physical work, you are not doing the job you are being paid to do. You are not delegating, not developing people, and most important, you are not leading. I am not criticizing management; I am simply pointing out the difference between doing physical work and managerial tasks. Appreciating the difference between the two and recognizing that the work you do as a manager is different from the physical work that your workers do will help you and your organization succeed.

MAPPING IT OUT

"If you do not know where you're going, any road will get you there." Lewis Carroll, Alice in Wonderland

Hard work alone will not get you to where you want to go, but working hard and working smart will. Setting goals is one of the smartest moves any entrepreneur can make. Establishing goals and planning how to reach them are critical to success. You need more than a target; you also need a plan. Your plan is a roadmap, just like the North Star provided a map for travelers before the invention of the magnetic compass. The compass has since been replaced by satellites and global positioning systems (GPSs), but, fortunately or unfortunately, GPSs are not designed to help users reach career goals. What we need is a PGD (personal guidance device), but this has yet to be invented. I will talk more about the essential elements of personal guidance in the coming paragraphs.

Goals are your internal compass. They help keep you on track and heading in the right direction. Goals help you stay focused on what is important, without becoming distracted. Setting goals is similar to planning a journey. You have to be specific about where you want to go. Goals have to be measurable and have to be attainable.

Like the mode of transportation you select for a journey, proper resources need to be in place for you to reach your goals and your goals must be consistent with your core values. It helps to visualize your goals and how you will achieve them - whatever your goals might be (that is, visualizing paying for your children's education, buying a new car, planning a trip to paradise, or launching a successful business). Use your imagination; it is a powerful incentive to work hard to achieve your goals. As Walt Disney once said, "If you dream it, you can do it. Always remember this started with a dream and a mouse."

Just as important as it is to set goals, it is equally important to avoid being myopic about them (that is, the journey that you take to achieve your goals is also important). Be sure to enjoy the process and recognize it is okay to take a detour from time to time, as long as you avoid getting sidetracked and ending up in the ditch or in the weeds. If you find yourself getting lost or losing sight of your goals, attend a seminar, take in a conference, benchmark with peers, or reconnect with a mentor. Remember, you do not have to be a Christopher Columbus-like trailblazer. I am almost embarrassed to admit there was a time when I thought I was the only one charting new territories. To my surprise, there were others, plenty of others, who had traveled the same path and made the same journey who were more than willing to share their experiences and recommendations. That is when I realized the power of networking.

Is it not true that getting smarter or educated is the most difficult part of any new activity? The first day on a new job, the first day of school, and the first step toward starting a new venture are all stressful times, characterized by moving into the unknown and being full of doubts. Will my boss accept me? Will my new teacher like me? Will customers buy from me? These questions, these challenges are real and the odds are against those who fail to look at them as opportunities.

WHATEVER IT TAKES

By the above definition of work, I had not been doing much of it for the decade prior to starting my lawncare business in 1994. I was like an athlete who moves into a management position (as did Michael Jordan with the Washington Wizards) and tries to make a comeback, but I was not a Michael Jordan. When I started my new venture, I was 50 years old. I may not have been the oldest lawn tech in the field, but I was in rare company as few people launch new businesses and careers at this stage in their lives. Because I came into the green industry late in my career, it was a major shift in my life. My pre-career employment resume started on the family farm, included some summers working as a roofer, a short stint as a factory worker, and as a teaching associate at The Ohio State University. My first career job was as an entry-level research technologist in research and development with Campbell Soup Company. Sixteen years later, I left Campbell Soup, as Vice President, R&D International, to become the Vice President of R&D at RJR Tobacco Company.

After almost 25 years in the corporate world, I had reached one of the highest R&D positions in the consumer products industry. I had 400 direct reports, a $40 million annual budget, a corner office with a view, a company car, a country club membership, and all the associated benefits of being a corporate officer in a relatively small town. This all abruptly changed in the early 1990s as RJR Industries adjusted to the aftermath of its colossal leveraged buyout by Kohlberg Kravis Roberts & Co. A process of executive musical chairs started, and when the music stopped, my expensive executive leather chair was gone and I had nowhere to sit.

What a turnaround from being on the short list to replace my boss to the blackball list after an outsider was hired. Even though I had a soft landing relative to financial issues, it was a direct body blow to my ego and self-image. It was a real punch in the nose to my psyche. At first I did not know what I wanted to do next - the only thing about which I was certain was I did not want another corporate job. Not that this was a major sacrifice - as mergers, buyouts, and economic contractions took their toll on consumer product companies, R&D management positions were becoming as extinct as saber tooth tigers.

I loved being in R&D and especially product development. It was exciting, hard work both physically and mentally. There was always something new to work on; actually, that was the name of the game! It was rewarding and frustrating all at the same time, but, as I advanced from a research technologist to the VP level, I found that the higher the position, the less the feeling of accomplishment. Not only was there a loss of the sense of achievement in the rarified air of a corporate suite, it was not much fun. There were large trade-offs involved. The honest, hands-on frustration of struggling with the development of a new process or product was traded for the maddening irritation of dealing with all of the corporate-hierarchy politics.

One fellow executive once told me that the way to survive in the corporate world was to develop an ability to distinguish the dolphins from the sharks: "Dolphins you can swim with; sharks eat you!" Dealing with colossal egos became an art form in survival - and that was just for my once or twice weekly visits to corporate headquarters. In R&D, a whole new set of rules applied. Almost everyone had to have either a Ph.D. or another advanced technical degree. Every professional was there because he or she was world-class in his or her respective technical or scientific expertise. Most not only thought they were superior, they were convinced of it. The egos were challenging, but the continuous, mind-numbing meetings were the killers. There were meetings to schedule meetings, meetings to plan meetings, and meetings to reduce meetings. I had so many meetings that the primary function of my secretary was to schedule, coordinate, and point me in the direction of the next meeting. Most meetings were unnecessary, nonproductive, and a boring waste of time - so boring in some cases that the most challenging aspect of the meetings was staying awake!

Unfortunately all this meeting attending did not prepare me well to start a company from scratch; I was completely out of shape. Oh, I ran three miles every day and did my sit-ups and pushups, but the physical - not to mention the emotional - strain was nearly overwhelming. The hard, often dirty, work was made more challenging by bulky spray pumps, electric reels that didn't reel, and vehicles that were not always reliable (we started with a lot of used equipment prone to breakdowns.)

I went out on customer calls for three primary reasons. First, as a new business owner, I was chronically short-handed and to get jobs done required help - my help. Second, I wanted to learn the business at the ground level so I could gain a better understanding of the equipment and turf issues at literally the ground, root level, including weeds, insects, and diseases. Finally, working in both good and difficult conditions, I wanted to gain firsthand knowledge of my customers and their lawns and gardens. Without question, I learned quickly that I could get a larger dose of reality in a hurry by talking face-to-face with customers in their front yards rather than discussing questions, issues, and complaints at arm's length on the telephone or over e-mail.

I mentioned feeling a degree of psychological and emotional strain. A good part of that came from suffering a bruised ego and being in shock of actually having to get my hands dirty rather than giving orders from an air conditioned office. I had to do every job - no matter how humbling. I swallowed my pride and set my sights on building a lawncare company one job at a time - just as a building contractor constructs a house one brick at a time. The mortar that held together the parts and connected the little jobs to the overall accomplishment was humility and the willingness to do whatever it took to build a lasting structure - my company, my career.

This reminds me of what I consider to be a funny story. Living and working in a relatively small city such as Winston-Salem, I was always seeing former colleagues from my previous employer. Some were supervisors and many more were former direct reports. The exchanges were always friendly, and we usually reminisced about old times and mutual friends. Upon seeing me, I am certain that many of my old acquaintances would stop and do double takes, observing a person who had traded in his suit and tie for blue jeans, work boots and gloves. As it were, many former colleagues became clients of mine, and I never really considered the irony of my working for them on their lawns until an old friend of mine recently told me about something that happened one fall about 12 to 14 years ago. I was heading up a crew that was aerating and seeding the lawn of a former employee who happened to be home at the time. According to my friend, this client had gotten a big kick out of watching me work and had said to my friend, "Life is good." I find this funny because life was good - for me. We billed this client $400 for the job, and that was only one of probably six jobs I completed that day. Furthermore, I was having a great time working outdoors, driving a tractor, and enjoying the fresh air helping Nature's Select grow one client at a time to become the largest and most successful privately owned lawncare company in the region. Ironically, today, that same client is unfortunately in an uncertain job situation with nowhere to go. Yes, life is good if you are willing to be humble and make sacrifices.

Sacrifices

An acorn when planted in the ground takes time to germinate and grow into a magnificent tree. The growing sapling needs nutrients, moisture, and protection before it becomes full-grown and can stand on its own. When starting a new enterprise, humility and sacrifice nurture the new organization. When Burt Sperber started ValleyCrest, cash flow was so tight that he would sometimes have to forgo paying himself to be able to make payroll. This was not a one-time occurrence and made balancing the home budget a challenge for his wife. However, the sacrifice was much appreciated by his employees who later helped to build Sperber's Southern California-based company into one of the world's premier green-industry companies.

Sperber had relatively few career options as a 19-year-old in the late

1940s. He could have continued to sell newspapers and to work for others, but he chose to follow his passion for plants and working outdoors and purchased a nursery business from the widow of his boss. This was not the case of Jennifer Lemcke.

Jennifer Lemcke had just graduated from college and was happily employed in a career-building job, when her father asked her and her husband to join his lawncare business. She traded the comfort and security of a high-tech office job to drive a lawncare service truck, pull a spray hose, and push a fertilizer spreader. It was a scary proposition for her to give up a well-paying position that she loved for the risky proposition of joining a new business venture - a real leap of faith for a person whose first experience in the lawncare business, as a 12-year-old telemarketer, was a teary failure. The reason she was willing to make this sacrifice was to be part of a family business and ultimately be her own boss. She relates that after the first year of extremely hard work when she figured her income was equivalent to three dollars per hour, she did entertain some second thoughts. Years later as she looks back, from her position as COO of Turf Holdings, Inc. (the owner of the franchise rights to the Weed Man name in the United States), she realizes that all of the hard work and sacrifices were worth it.

No matter if you are the founder or an employee of an enterprise, there are certain personal character factors that the successful professional entrepreneur must possess and two of the most critical are the willingness to make sacrifices for the long-term and have a sense of humility.

HUMILITY

One of the silver heads at Campbell Soup Company at the launch of a major new product made the following remark, "The key to our success is humility." Being new with the company at the time and inexperienced in working with teams executing large projects, I did not appreciate or understand what this experienced executive was trying to say. It was not until many years later when I started Nature's Select that I comprehended his message. Maintaining a sense of humility is hard work and requires discipline. It is every bit as hard to exercise control over one's ego as it is to physically dig ditches. You may not get blisters on your hands, but it definitely requires the expenditure of a lot of energy!

Learning from Failure

One of the more difficult lessons in life is learning that it is not the end of the world if you fail at something, especially if you make the mistake early on, while trying something new. In fact, failing to fail can have severe consequences.

Here is a case in point - one I call Hannah and the bicycle. Hannah is my 11-year old granddaughter who is approaching voting age intellectually but seems much younger in terms of coordination and physical ability. She was born three-months premature and struggled early on with balance and physical strength. For several years, she had been trying to learn to ride a bicycle. Unfortunately, when she first started down this road to master an important rite-of-passage, she took a nasty spill - one that catapulted her over the handlebars and literally took the air out of her confidence. She was equipped with helmet and kneepads, so the spill did not hurt her physically, but the fall impacted her confidence and the fear of failure slowed her progress. Hannah has a strong will and persisted. Today she proudly rides her bicycle. The moral of this story is a simple, albeit, an important one: you have to get up after a failure or mistake, learn from the experience, and move forward. What if Hannah failed to fail? What if she mastered her bicycle without any mishap? Chances are the training wheels would have come off before she was ready, and it would have been full speed ahead down the driveway straight into a privet hedge. She might have gotten away with a few minor scrapes or bruises or suffered a more serious injury with broken bones. This is what happened to her grandfather decades earlier.

As a young boy during the late 1940s and early '50s, a bike represented freedom and individual expression. Running into hedges and jumping over standing objects caused me little if any fear. Getting hit by a car was, however, a different story. I can still vividly recall the day when I was riding my bike to a friend's house to trade baseball cards. My mind was on the forthcoming transactions when I peddled through a stop sign without looking. The next thing I knew, I was superman, flying through the air - but superman in mind only. Trying to avoid me, the car skidded to a stop, smacking my conveyance squarely in the side. I flew across the street and did not come close to touching the ground until I hit the curb. By that time, though, my momentum had slowed, and the crash resulted only in a sprained ankle - and a mangled bicycle. Now, if I had experienced what Hannah experienced at her young age, I might have had more respect for one's vulnerability while riding a bike. No, instead I learned the hard way, but, at least, lived to tell the story.

I learned another hard lesson later in life while working for Campbell Soup as a junior R&D food technologist. I had been on the job only a month, when my boss came to me with a unique problem. The company's new pet division was introducing a line of canned dog food. Campbell Soup had advertised for years on the Lassie Show and now wanted to promote a new dog food. The product was to be a canned meatball stew, topped off with a chew biscuit.

This was a clever gimmick developed by the company's marketing arm and an outside ad agency, but it turned into a nightmare riddled with technical and production obstacles. The challenge was to produce a chew biscuit that would retain its shape while the dog food was being sterilized. A traditional biscuit simply turned into mush, so the R & D department had come up with a biscuit coated with an oil resin that prevented moisture from entering the biscuit. Unfortunately, the solution doubled the processing time, and its tacky characteristic meant the production workers and not machines would have to place the biscuit into the cans. Consequently, to launch the new Lassie dog food, the biscuit idea was going to cost Campbell Soup millions of dollars more than anticipated.

So there I was, new on the job with my first major assignment. At first, I was not pleased because I had turned down a higher paying position with the Quaker Oats' pet food division. I wanted to work with human food, not dog food! The new pet food division was, however, desperate. The test market was a success and Lassie and the product had already been on a photo shoot. Management was anxious to go into production, but the projected cost was prohibitive.

Seven years of college will train you for almost anything, but not making heat resistant chew biscuits. My assistant and I took the original resin formula and mixed up a batch. Everything that touched the resin was destroyed; it set so stone solid that even jack hammers could not remove it from the mixing utensils! Stumped, I asked myself how nature would solve this problem. Well, a real dog bone is comprised of a complex matrix of minerals with a protein lattice. We went back to the drawing board and added protein, including wheat gluten and bone meal to our formula. Voilá, we had a treat that held its shape. Because it bounced like a super ball should have been an early warning sign, but it was not. My boss, however, noted that the color was slightly off, so we added beta carotene. The color was perfect and because beta carotene is a precursor to Vitamin A, the company had something else to promote with Lassie on the label.

Everyone was happy - my boss, his bosses, and virtually everyone affiliated with the new division. We were heroes, and now all we had to do was go into biscuit production. For a trial run, we borrowed some time on the assembly line at a nearby Pepperidge Farms facility. Between two shifts, we confidently mixed up the batter. There again, we should have had another inkling that something was wrong; the amps on the mixing motor were maxing out. We forged ahead, though, and placed the dough between the rollers (the machine was called a rotary mold unit) and flipped the switch. Almost immediately, there was a huge bang, and bolts started to shear off the master roller.

Oh boy, were we in trouble, now - from being heroes to being in the dog house in less time than it takes the moon to change phases! The 24-hour production line was shut down and we did not have a clue how to solve the problem, which we later determined stemmed from having too much protein in our formula. The gluten matrix had an elastic trait that caused the dough to actually "snap back" to its original shape. Well, after tinkering with the formula - taking out some protein here and some minerals there, we eventually came up with a chew biscuit that held its shape and did not destroy the forming machinery.

Yes, we eventually worked out the dilemma, but, trust me, it would have been a whole lot easier on both my assistant and me if we had worked out the production problems in the pilot plant before shutting down an entire "goldfish" factory. The point is, early failure is not all bad. Making mistakes (all part of the learning curve) can prove valuable for young children riding bicycles, upstart R & D technologists, and even entrepreneurs.

THE PROCESS OF PROBLEM SOLVING

One relatively rare key to success is the ability to solve problems on the fly. Some individuals are intuitive problem-solvers. Most people, though, have to develop this skill. If you can solve a problem better than a competitor, you have a competitive advantage.

I have always approached problem solving in a rather simple manner. As I commented above, I say to myself, "How would Mother Nature" solve the problem. Here are four examples:

- Lassie Recipe Dog Food - formulated a retort-stable chew biscuit fortified with protein and minerals.
- Created the first patented semi-dry pet food resembling a bone slice.
- Using all natural ingredients, developed Prego spaghetti sauce -

the first home-style, naturally-thick sauce.
- Founded Nature's Select Premium Turf Services, Inc. based on providing biologically-based, plant healthcare programs for grass, ornamentals, and large trees.

In the final analysis, solving problems is simply hard work. It takes a combination of discipline, focused technical ability, and the willingness to become submerged in the details until a solution is reached. There is no shortcut or magic trick to facilitate this process. Professionals realize this, roll up their sleeves, and attack the problem head-on.

Discipline

When I went to work for Campbell Soup, style points were not awarded for wearing the best clothes, driving the fanciest cars, or living in the most luxurious homes. It became obvious early on I had to quickly produce and add value for a company that generated a slim three percent margin on its food products. There was not much room for error and appearances were secondary.

Discipline was so engrained - from the general offices in New Jersey to company plants and locations around the country - that everyone fell in line with no questions asked. Those who did not adapt did not last. The pervasiveness of this thinking, in combination with my inexperience, allowed me to drink the "Kool Aid" completely. It was not until several years later sitting in my boss's office that I confronted this thinking head on. The meeting occurred after the completion of an exceptionally complicated and difficult project.

My boss said to me, "Bill, congratulations on finishing this project. Of course, you know why you and your team succeeded, don't you? Discipline was the key and it's always the key to getting something done."

While listening to this impromptu lecture, I said to myself, "Boy, are you nuts. Do you realize the technical hoops we jumped through to complete this job? Do you realize the long hours we put in and the number of reformulations we tried? I literally traveled around the world to find solutions to finish this project. Discipline had nothing to do with it. If he thinks this was how the job was done, he is badly misinformed." This must be a common reaction between bosses and their subordinates because today the roles have been reversed, and I see my employees looking at me quizzically when I suggest they need to become more disciplined. Little did I realize that those hoops and hours were exactly what he was defining as "discipline."

Years later, I viewed this moment as one of the watershed learning experiences of my life. With so much experience under his belt, my boss knew that the only way to overcome obstacles and complete tough tasks was through rock hard discipline. With all the distractions of the world we live in today, without strong mental and physical discipline, it is difficult - no, it is nearly impossible - to stay on task, let alone complete a task.

The great thing is that discipline, unlike dedication, can be learned. Behavioral scientists may disagree with me, but I think dedication is something innate within one's personality or makeup. Discipline, on the other hand, can be taught; reference how the Marine Corps can forge a group of undisciplined and raw young men and women into a tightly run unit.

Few companies today are run like the Marine Corps or even like the executives of Campbell Soup Company ran their company in the 1970s. How do employees of the owners of green industry companies become more disciplined? It begins with self-awareness and understanding what my boss told me early on - that discipline is critical to performing and completing difficult tasks.

We can also learn by studying successful entrepreneurs and understanding how they overcome difficulties. Attending a trade association conference or workshop, starting a peer group, signing up for a local community college course on the subject are great ways of interacting with other entrepreneurs. Even Teddy Roosevelt and Winston Churchill were not always great; they each overcame tremendous challenges through the practice of discipline. Reading their works can be inspiring. Later I present additional insights that I have learned from these heroic leaders.

Motivation

"Ability is what you're capable of doing. Motivation determines what you do. Attitude determines how well you do it." - Lou Holtz

Motivating Oneself

"Oh, I just don't feel like going to work, today. I guess I'll call in sick." That's a luxury that most entrepreneurs cannot afford. Sure, if you are down and out and cannot walk and talk, you cannot work, but by and large, persons who own and run their own companies are motivated to get to work. If you are thinking about starting a company, stop right now if you are not a self-starter.

For all the long hours and hard work that it takes to start up, manage and maintain a business, you need to have a high level of motivation. There are no cheerleaders on the sidelines rooting for you to get out of bed and tackle the everyday challenges of a small business operation. Motivation is not a 9 to 5 deal; it is not shift work; and it cannot be turned off once you leave work. It is a fixed state of mind that originates from a deep set of core values.

Can a person be too motivated? At first blush, this may seem like a strange question. Indeed, can a person be too good looking, too smart, or too nice? Still, there is no question that being around hyper-motivated individuals can be a real drag. They are often involved in frenzied activities and can burn out well before the jobs are completed. I compare these people to Fourth of July fireworks that are quick to rise, erupt in a tremendous display of brilliance, explode, and quickly fade away on the way back to earth (reality).

Sometimes enthusiasm is mistaken for motivation. There is, however, a difference between an enthusiastic person shouting encouragement from the sideline and a person who is motivated and playing the game. As a soccer coach for my children, I always found it curious how severely overweight parents would shout from the sidelines for their children to move and play harder. Sometimes it is difficult to know whether a person is too motivated, or just overly enthusiastic. In either case there is a large bang with limited lasting results.

Motivation comes in many forms and originates from many different sources, positive and/or negative. Throughout our lives, we encounter "big-men wannabes," those who suffer from small statures (Napoleon-like personalities). Roosevelt and Churchill had physical shortcomings early in their lives, and this probably helped inspire them to greater things, to become 'Michael Jordans' of politics. By the way, Michael Jordan did not even make his high school basketball team when he first tried out for it.

In nature, there is a phenomenon known as sublimation, which is the process whereby a solid such as ice passes directly into a gas without first going through a liquid phase. This can be observed on a cold morning, when the car window defroster is turned on and the thin layer of frost appears to magically disappear. In human psychology, this term is used to describe the conversion of negative energy into a positive force. An example would be a person who loses a bid to a competitor, channels the disappointment into improving the company's operating efficiency, and becomes a more successful contractor in the long run. When it works, sublimation is the ultimate coping mechanism. Even when you are not leveraging its positive benefits, understanding sublimation can help you recognize when you are being affected by the corrosive effects of negative thought.

No one knows for sure how much superstars have been motivated by early failures and shortcomings, and/or loss and revenge. I think, however, that these negative motivators generally require too much energy to sustain motivation in the long term. A marathon runner is better off running the distance with positive thoughts banging around in his head rather than trying to get to the finish line fueled by negative thoughts the entire way. How often have we heard athletes describe their visualizing good performances and victories? I cannot remember hearing an athlete describing visualizations of bad performances and defeat.

I think of positive motivation as a high performance engine. Most of the time it is on autopilot or cruise control, running at a constant RPM sufficient to climb minor hills and dodge pot holes. When a major detour or obstacle appears, the four-barrel carburetor kicks in and the extra power (motivation) gets the job done. The engine revs up for a period of time and then settles back down into a smooth rhythm. No excesses, no out-of-control spinouts and no red-lining of the engine - just a smooth transition of power.

Motivating Others

As challenging as motivating oneself is, it is a different ballgame when it comes to motivating others. How do you motivate and reward people to do good work without de-incentivizing them? I am still trying to figure this out, and, actually, it may be easier to determine the origins of life and whether or not it exists outside our solar system than to develop a unifying theory on motivation. Perhaps this is not as difficult a problem as discovering proof for the Big Bang theory or locating black holes, but for us mortals, it is damned difficult. This difficulty has not, however, prevented people from presenting their ideas on how people can and should be motivated. In 1776, Adam Smith published the book ***The Wealth of Nations*** in which he planted the seeds for capitalism and free market thinking. He stressed that competition is best for society and predicted that the division of labor (assembly line work) would improve production and eliminate inefficiencies in the manufacture of goods, but he also cautioned that this division of labor would reduce humans to "stupid and ignorant creatures." A hundred years later, in his book ***Capital*** (1870), Karl Marx expanded on this theme and stated, "From each man according to his ability, to each according to his need." He was saying that in his vision of a utopian society, people would consume only what they needed without regard to what they contributed. The great communist experiment of the 20th century that took place in Russia and China does not support Marx's thinking. Toward the end of the 20th Century, millions of people were living in poverty with diminished expectations and living standards, and this continues in places such as North Korea.

In ***The General Theory of Employment, Interest, and Money*** (1937) John Keynes argued that capitalistic economics needed government intervention to help recover from cyclical downturns. He strongly believed "a somewhat comprehensive socialization of investments" was necessary by governments to stabilize the monetary systems of nations. Keynes wrote his book while observing the behavior of governments during the great worldwide depression of the 1930s.

In her popular book ***Atlas Shrugged*** published in 1957, Ayn Rand expanded on her vision of a technological utopia based on laissez-faire capitalism and individualism. She contends that people are best motivated by self-interest. Large incentives, she wrote, motivate people to make sacrifices and take risks for their own self-improvement - thereby improving society in the process. Her vision is the polar opposite of what Marx had professed almost 90 years earlier.

During the last 200 years, there have been numerous theories about the best way to motivate people, and the jury is still out. On the surface, it would appear that capitalism has won. Economic systems are, however, constantly evolving, and the recent worldwide economic downturn has forced governments to take decidedly socialistic steps in attempts to stabilize key industries. It is difficult to relate the suggestions of Marx, Smith, Keynes and Rand to everyday business operations and to use these suggestions to somehow better motivate employees. Fortunately, there are recent, practical suggestions that are more helpful.

Theory X and Y

After World War II, Harvard University established the field of industrial social psychology. One of the prominent professors of the time was Douglas McGregor of the Massachusetts Institute of Technology, Sloan School of Management. In his book ***The Human Side of Enterprise***, he introduced the X and Y theories of worker motivation. Theory X assumed that workers and the population in general were inherently lazy and would avoid work; therefore, a strong command-and-control type of management was necessary to achieve productive work. Theory Y assumed the exact opposite - that people are self motivated, want to be productive, and would assume responsibility when given the opportunity.

Over the years, both theories have undergone major rethinking and positioning as evidenced by the evolution of business management practices. The military hierarchal structure, so popular in the 1950s, was replaced by the Japanese-style, total quality management, which was inspired by Dr. W. Edwards Deming. More recently, companies have adopted the lean-management principles developed by Toyota. Thanks to the Ariens Company and JP Horizons, the enlightened management concepts of reducing waste and engaging employees at all levels have been introduced to a large number of companies in the green industry. Through his Optimum Provision Management program, Robert Hayter of The Hayter Firm has applied these principles at the landscaper crew level. How business leaders view and operate their companies today is the result of the evolution of manufacturing management practices since World War II. My personal worker motivation theory can be symbolized by the letter W, which is a combination of the X and Y theories. Depending on the circumstances workers (or people in general) demonstrate both X and Y characteristics. Some people at work are Ys, but after hours they become Xs! And vice versa!

MOTIVATORS THAT DO NOT MOTIVATE

Many institutions have conducted extensive research on what motivates people and what incentives actually produce positive behavior. The results of many of these studies are counterintuitive. Here are two examples:

During a blood-shortage crisis, an agency devised a plan to pay donors to give blood. The pay-for-blood campaign backfired when the number of donors dramatically decreased. In follow-up interviews, it was discovered that the main motivation for giving blood was that it made people feel good to contribute to a worthy cause. The positive psychological benefits disappeared when people were paid for their blood. The agency stopped offering to pay for blood and focused their marketing efforts on volunteer altruism.

In Israel, parents were not picking up their children from a day-care center at the designated time. The tardiness resulted in overtime hours for the workers and created major scheduling difficulties. The day-care center responded by imposing a $15 fine for every 15 minutes the parents were late in picking up their children. The opposite of the desired action occurred. Instead of being encouraged by the fines to pick up their children on time, tardy parents thought that if they were paying for the additional time they were not obliged to be on time.

Both of the above stories demonstrate that money is not always the strongest incentive to achieve a desired result.

An MIT study about rewarding technical and engineering workers in the high tech industry also found the same result. It seems that being recognized by peers for technical expertise was more powerful than a monetary bonus. The best incentive was to be permitted (or asked) to present a technical paper in front of work colleagues or at a professional conference. Attending conferences and trade shows also provided the added incentive of networking and learning about the latest developments within the industry.

Tracy Kidder in his 1981 Pulitzer Prize winning book ***Soul of a***

New Machine follows a team of Data General Corporation engineers developing an innovative new computer. What Mr. Kidder discovered in his year-long observation was that the greatest motivator for doing extremely difficult, frustrating, and demanding work was simply an unspoken promise: "If you do good work you will be assigned to the next big project and get to do it all over again!" This is what defines a professional - you must love your work and doing good work in itself ensures that you will get to continue to do the job you love!

This approach may work for engineers, but not for typical green industry workers (in my case lawncare technicians). Motivating them requires more than a promise to have the opportunity to do the same job day after day, week after week, and season after season. Yes, everyone is interested in job security, and when the employment rate is headed toward double-digits, it is even a stronger motivator. Job security diminishes as an incentive when the economy is strong and there are more relatively low-paying jobs than workers willing to put in the long hours and hard work they demand.

Cultural Revolution to Consumer Revolution

The largest social and economic experiment of all times was the communist revolution in 20th Century China. In 1984, while on a technology exchange tour sponsored by the National Academy of Sciences and the equivalent Chinese government agency, I had the rare privilege of a glimpse of old communist China. As a result of Richard Nixon's meetings with Mao Zedong (the Marxist leader of China), China was just starting to open up to the West. One of the outcomes of this diplomacy initiative was to exchange technology in critical areas such as transportation, energy, and food production. I was invited to travel to China to be part of the food technology exchange contingency.

China, in the mid-1980s, was still dominated by a strong Communist doctrine. In the cities the primary mode of transportation was the bicycle, and no private cars were to be seen. Billboards were used exclusively for government propaganda slogans. People dressed in nondescript clothing of gray and drab green monotones, and the stores had little or no consumer goods - just basic items. This included Shanghai, which at the time was the most cosmopolitan city in China. Our trip was shocking to us Americans, but it was even more shocking to the Chinese. Crowds formed around us several feet deep to just stare at us, as if we were some exotic species from another world - this in retrospect was figuratively true.

My most enduring memory of this trip was how subdued the spirit of the people seemed to be. The cumulative impacts of Mao's Great Leap Forward and later the Cultural Revolution were devastating. Schools and colleges were closed and intellectuals were attacked and disgraced. Remnants of these upheavals could be seen in the faces and demeanors of the people, but what seemed to most prominently permeate everyone's being was a lack of motivation and enthusiasm. When his shift was over, our bus driver stopped in the middle of the countryside, and the tour officer had to finish driving us to our destination. Sales clerks with their backs facing the customers leaned against half-filled display cases and ignored requests for assistance. People were at work, but no work was being done. This is what happens when people's spirits are restrained and there is no incentive to work hard and do a good job.

Only four years later, after restrictions had been eased and the transformation to limited capitalism was underway, I returned to China and observed that a massive change had occurred. Billboards advertising stores filled with consumer goods had replaced slogans, and there were friendly, helpful salespeople. The streets were bustling with brightly dressed and smiling people. On most blocks, there were construction projects. Today, 22 years later, China is an economic colossus rivaling the U.S. A funny thing happens to the human spirit and attitude when proper incentives are in place.

Involved/Engaged

Professional athletes perform their best when playing their chosen sports. They are fully engaged, and it shows. The same holds true in the business world. Professionals in business get dirty and bruised and share winning and losing with their team members.

Not all business people, however, get or stay engaged and instead sit in the stands and, like fans, watch from a distance as their team performs on the field. Even worse than the people in the stands are those who shout obscenities from the sidelines like observers did in the Coliseum during Roman times. We know what happened to the Romans.

My mantra is, "Get off the sidewalk and join the parade." Better yet, "Get off the sidewalk and lead the parade." Stay engaged. It is easy to disconnect when setbacks occur such as when you do not get the raise you expected or when you lose a big contract to a lower bidder. Successful professionals stay engaged and focused on making improvements in the face of adversity. They do not sulk, quit, nor otherwise turn off, and they know how to move on after setbacks. The professional focuses on how to use setbacks as learning tools. Abraham Lincoln had numerous setbacks in life, and he lost a lot of elections before he won the presidency. Despite the losses, he never gave up; he kept plugging away and learning from his mistakes and ultimately became one of the greatest U.S. presidents of all time. Babe Ruth grew up in what can best be described as a reform school and struck out thousands of times, but that did not discourage him from becoming the King of Swat.

Just like motivation, being engaged implies continuity of mindset. Successful professional athletes are not engaged part-time; part-time engagement does not work well in competitive environments. You cannot be engaged one day and be off to slackerville or Margaritaville the next. It does not work in professional sports, and it does not work in the business world. No amount of talent can overcome one's inability to stay engaged.

John Daly is one of the most talented golfers on the PGA tour, yet a lack of discipline to stay engaged has resulted in inconsistent play and put his touring card in jeopardy. Tiger Woods, on the other hand, has combined talent, hard work, discipline and total engagement to be one of the greatest sports figures of all time. Given Woods' recent personal indiscretions, only time will tell if he can regain the focus and discipline that carried him to the top of the golfing world.

MASTERING YOUR CRAFT

In ***Outliers, The Story of Success***, Malcolm Gladwell puts new emphasis on hard work as it relates to one's profession. The premise of Gladwell's book is it takes an investment of 10,000 hours to achieve mastery of your craft. To put this in perspective, 10,000 hours equals 3.4 years of effort - eight hours per day, seven days per week with no vacations or holidays. Obviously it is almost impossible to devote every waking moment to learning one's profession. There are other important skills that also have to be successfully learned to become a professional. To record the requisite 10,000 hours in a business context probably requires 10 years. The lesson here is that if people are going to reach extraordinary professional success, they usually need to start early. Bill Gates started as a teenage computer geek to become a software czar; after several years of playing in obscure strip clubs in Hamburg, Germany, the Beatles rose from an unknown Liverpool band to the most successful band of all time. The common theme is that these people all had talent, but it took years before they mastered their crafts and became world-class successes. The details may differ, but the same theme for success is evident in the careers of the entrepreneurs, business leaders, and educators included in this book.

The following stories support the theme that starting early and working hard are keys to becoming successful in business and becoming a professional:

- David Snodgrass, CEO of Seven Dees Landscaping, located in Portland, Oregon, knew that he would be taking over the family business when he was in the third grade, after the affirmation he received when he took his $0.35 earnings from watering plants at five cents per hour to show and tell. At this young age, he wanted to be a businessman. Working alongside his siblings and parents and majoring in marketing at Oregon State University, he learned every aspect of the nursery business. Dave now heads one of the largest nursery and landscaping organizations in the Northwest.

- Jennifer Lemke, CEO of Weed Man USA, was cold calling lawncare prospects at the age of 12 and is now CEO of Weed Man franchises in the US.
- Robert Hayter, a certified landscape architect and owner of a Pinehurst, North Carolina landscaping company, bought a lawnmower at nine years of age and started a lawn mowing service. Robert is now recognized as one of the foremost restoration landscape architects.
- Burt Sperber at the age of 19 took his earnings from years of working in a nursery and formed a partnership with his father to purchase his former boss's company for $700 and in the following 60 years grew the enterprise to $1 billion in annualized sales.

The take-home message is that there is no shortcut to success - it requires hard work. Timing, opportunity, and intelligence are important elements, but success rarely happens - and will not be sustained - without hard work. A maxim to live by: start early, work hard, stay late - it is not a job, it is a career!

The Question

When I was 10 years old, I asked my father why one of our neighbors owned so much acreage and was so successful at farming when both the father and the son did not seem all that smart. My dad looked at me and without pausing said, "Well, son, if you're willing to work hard enough, you can make up for almost any shortcoming." Noting my puzzled expression, he said, "Bill, just think what you can accomplish if you work hard and are smart at the same time!" Whenever I have to tackle a difficult problem, or take on a new project, and need inspiration, all I have to do is recall this little talk.

Hard work is important to a person's ultimate success; however, if it were the only element in the formula for success, then the Fortune 500 list would need to be increased to the Fortune 1000 because the numbers of successful enterprises would be growing exponentially. There are a lot of hard working people in this great big world we live in, but, unfortunately, there is much more that goes into the formula than just hard work.

The following homily is about the Olie the woodcutter who learned this lesson the hard way. This story was told to me many years ago and I have been unable to recall the name of the person who shared it, so the origins of the story are obscure and my apologies to the original author for borrowing his or her story without giving credit.

THE SAGA OF OLIE JOHANSEN THE NORWEGIAN WOODCUTTER

Olie was the prototypical old-world lumberjack from a long lineage of Norwegian woodsmen. Olie was 6'5", had a barrel chest, and had arms and hands made for swinging an axe. At age 26, he decided that his destiny was in the New World, so he made his way to the forests of Minnesota where he soon found a job working in a lumber camp. As the foreman explained to Olie, lumberjacks were paid by the number of trees they cut per day and totaled by the week. The pay scale was as follows: an experienced lumberjack could cut approximately 40 trees per day at $0.50 per tree, so during good weather, a skilled chopper could make $20 per day (unheard of wages in Norway). But what really got Olie's attention was that after 200 trees were cut in a 5-day week, any additional trees over this amount were paid at $1 per tree - incentive pay is not just a modern phenomenon!

So the next morning Olie awoke from dreaming about the riches he was about to earn and immediately went to work chopping down trees at a furious rate. At the end of the day, after continuous work with only small breaks for food and water, Olie had cut down 35 trees. If Olie was disappointed in not achieving his 40-tree goal on his first day, he did not show it. He was brimming with optimism and knew that his muscles would become more conditioned, that his tender hands would form calluses, and that he could do much better. The next morning with as much confidence as ever, he began the morning swinging his axe with more precision and snap - even though his muscles ached and red spots formed on his hands. By mid-afternoon, he was surprised, however, to learn he had cut down only 25 trees, so he redoubled his efforts skipping a water break and took comfort as a spring shower cooled this hot and perspiring body. At the end of the second day, his total tree count stood at or rather fell to 34. One less than the day before!

Olie was not a math prodigy, but he could add pretty well, and as he lay down to sleep that night, he tallied 69 trees cut down for approximately a $35 paycheck–not bad he thought, but he realized that if he were to make his bonus, he would have to cut 131 trees in three days (44 trees per day) to achieve the 200-tree threshold. As he fell asleep, he vowed to get up earlier (before the sun came up), to redouble his efforts, and to work until the sun set. His pride would not let him be deterred from reaching his goal of 200+ trees for the week and obtaining the one-dollar-per-tree bonus. On day three, even though he was true to his pre-slumber vows, his total again slipped. Olie was becoming frustrated. With only two days left, he was more behind. He started the fourth day with a vengeance - he spoke to no one, skipped lunch and breaks, and was muttering a curse with every swing. At the end of the day, when the foreman posted the daily count, Olie was almost blind with rage - his count had fallen to a dismal 28 trees. He was not in last place on the lumber-camp leader board - that distinction belonged to the cook who went out to cut trees during his off hours only!

Friday morning was a combination of frustrations, bruised muscles, bleeding hands, and wounded pride. Almost in tears by noontime, after being able to conquer only 10 trees, Olie went to his foreman for advice. The foreman gave Olie a quick once over, noted his bent shoulders and blistered hands and asked Olie one question,

"Olie, by any chance, have you sharpened your axe lately?"

The moral of the story is that you can be the most dedicated and hard worker, but if you do not take the time to sharpen the tools with which you work, you will not achieve your goals.

In the remaining chapters and interviews of this book, I attempt to identify some of the characteristics that go into making successful entrepreneurs and professionals.

"If I had eight hours to chop down a tree, I'd spend six hours sharpening my axe." – Abraham Lincoln

CHAPTER III

Personal Character

"Character is like a tree and a reputation like its shadow, the shadow is what we think of it, the tree is the real thing." Abraham Lincoln

Like many words, "character" can have multiple meanings and can mean different things to different people. That is what makes our language fun, right? Take the word "behave." When a mother's children are misbehaving, she may think that she is making a reasonable, modest request when she admonishes her children to behave. From the children's perspective, they may think that they are behaving, so asking them to behave is redundant or they may think the request is unreasonable in that it is a request for super-natural restraint.

The same difference in perception may occur when considering personal character. There are multiple facets of peoples' characters and these are often judged differently by different people. Of course, some people are just plain "characters", and some people (such as the following presidents) had such strong and prominent personal character traits that they become part of their identities:

- Honest Abe Lincoln
- Stonewall Jackson
- Old-Hickory Andrew Jackson
- Rough-Riding Teddy Roosevelt
- Give-'em-hell Harry Truman

In an age of intense media scrutiny, modern presidents have found that less favorable character traits have come to define them:

- Tricky Dickie Nixon
- Teflon Ronald Reagan
- Slick-Willie Clinton

PERSONAL INTEGRITY

In my opinion, the most important professional character traits a person can have are honesty and trustworthiness. If people cannot be trusted, without regard to their educations/skills, they are not complete professionals. It was the work of intelligent, but flawed and incomplete professionals who lead to the collapse of Enron, and more recently, the financial and housing market downturn. Would you go to a gifted physician who had a reputation for insurance fraud or malpractice? I certainly would not, nor would I want to be associated with any professional whom I could not trust. One of the best compliments that a person can receive is that he or she has high personal integrity.

"KNOW THYSELF" – PLATO

Can you be trusted? Are you honest and straightforward? You almost certainly think so, but these are relative terms, and so the real question is what do the people around you think. One of the most difficult things for people to understand in both their personal and professional lives is how others perceive them. Peoples' opinions of themselves may be completely at odds with how they are perceived by family, friends, and business colleagues. We all know individuals who have inflated opinions of themselves (we all fall into this trap at one time or another), and we know people who underestimate themselves. In most cases, there is a difference between what we think about ourselves and what other people think about us. Spending time to understand what others think about us can help us change inaccurate perceptions and may even give us insight into areas for self-improvements.

Self-perception is determined by many factors - a reflection in the mirror, social status, skill set, personality, education level, feedback from others, etc. Having an accurate understanding of your self is a challenge. You must be able to recognize your strong points, acknowledge areas of weakness, and be sensitive to your impact on other people.

Core Values As Solid As Granite

Many components generally go into the formation of one's character. Dave Zerfoss, formerly the president of Husqvarna USA, describes this process as a combination of events large and small, starting with a person's earliest memories. For Dave, it was growing up on a small farm with his parents and older brother, Danny, and learning to appreciate the small things in life. Here he developed core values as solid as the granite from his home state of Pennsylvania.

Zerfoss's formative years were a synthesis of farm, church and school activities. Among these, farm work and church attendance were the dominant forces. Elementary and high school were important factors, but what most shaped Dave's character was working alongside his father and brother and participating in church functions. Dave credits the family's custom-harvesting service with introducing him to the art of relationship building. He met interesting people from around the country and worked alongside them. During strawberry season, not only did Dave pick strawberries, but he also helped his dad load the truck and go to town to sell the strawberries door-to-door. His dad worked one side of the street while Dave worked the other. This is where Zerfoss learned to overcome the fear of a "cold call", a talent that paid big dividends in his first paying job after college. Dave relays that you have to knock on a lot of doors to sell a truckload of strawberries!

Acknowledge Your Weaknesses, Enhance Your Strengths

Knowing, accepting, and even embracing who you are is critical to your personal development. If you have weaknesses, do not try to camouflage or deny their existence, but focus instead on how you can improve these areas or mitigate their impact. Teddy Roosevelt and Winston Churchill, both born with high social status and privilege, were physically weak and sickly as children, and there were doubts as to whether or not they would live through their teenage years. Through sheer determination and iron discipline, however, they overcame their physical handicaps to become two of the greatest leaders of the 20th Century.

The finest and strongest steel is forged in the hottest fire. As children, the future President Roosevelt and the future Prime Minister Churchill had internal fires that burned in their guts. Through strenuous workouts and feats of daring, they were relentless in overcoming their adolescent physical limitations. They were convinced that they could overcome weak muscles and respiratory problems through sheer determination and will power. One even wonders if the foundation of their future success was laid as they honed the mental strengths required to overcome these physical deficiencies.

A realistic assessment of your limitations and acknowledgement of what you cannot do are important. It is also important to know what you can do. Michael Phelps has proven himself to be the best human swimmer of all time. His record-setting eight gold medals at the Beijing Olympics will likely stand for a long time. He has the physical features that make him a natural swimmer - long body and arms, large hands, and a huge lung capacity. In essence, he is a human fish.

Yet, with all these superior physical attributes, he probably would not even be able to perform at the college level if he played football or even basketball. Had Michael decided on pursuing any of these other sports, he would likely have been a "fish out of water." If another Michael by the name of Jordan at first had tried to pursue a pro baseball versus basketball career, there certainly would never have been 'Air Jordan' sneakers selling for premium prices around the world.

Once you have determined the strengths to focus on and have either improved on or shielded your weaknesses, set realistic goals. If you're not over six feet tall, it's going to be difficult to make it in the NBA even though you may be a great dribbler with a sweet three-point shot. Giving up eight inches in height is difficult to overcome when the competition is also likely to have a well-developed skill set. It is important to be honest with yourself and be sensitive to the perceptions of others. Be comfortable in your own skin, feel good about yourself, and have confidence and the courage to leverage your abilities. Success will occur naturally.

Returning to Dave Zerfoss - after attending a one-room schoolhouse for five years, Dave advanced to the "big school" located in the nearest town. Here he was placed in the academic track; however, compared to his brother Danny, who later attended Harvard on a full scholarship and became a renowned professor in medieval history at the University of Delaware, Dave did not feel particularly gifted intellectually. One talent did become apparent, however. In Dave's activities within the church, he proved to be a natural public speaker, and he soon found himself giving presentations at youth conferences and rising to a leadership position within the church. Only later did he realize it was a special gift to be able to influence people through communication, and it is a skill that he has continually worked hard to perfect.

The following characteristics come together to create your unique character portrait.

Openness

Be receptive to new ideas and people. Reciprocate by sharing your thoughts and ideas. Do not allow hidden agendas or secret motives handicap your relations with others. A sense of humor and a smile enhance open discussion and a relaxed atmosphere. Having an attitude or a closed mind prevent an open exchange of ideas and discourages sharing. An excellent technique that can be learned easily is to always begin a critique of a new idea by saying something positive. Remember, a closed vessel allows nothing to escape or to enter.

STRAIGHTFORWARDNESS

Avoid dancing around issues. Instead, deal with facts in a straightforward manner and try not to embellish. Time is one of the most important resources that you have, and much of it can be wasted communicating with subtleties and nuances - not to mention the damage that can be caused by misunderstandings. Jack Friday from the 1950s TV show Dragnet was famous for saying, "Just the facts ma'am, just the facts." This saying is applicable today when professionals are involved in discussions.

"Let your Discourse with Men of Business be Short and Comprehensive."
George Washington, Rules of Civility

This is sound advice from our first president and is as true today as it was when President Washington was managing his business affairs from Mount Vernon in the late 1700s. Many sales and opportunities are lost by people who talk too much and do not listen.

CULTURAL AND REGIONAL DIFFERENCES

I learned early in my adult life to be aware of cultural and regional differences - lessons that are appropriate for both social and business settings. For centuries, the United States has been called the Great Melting Pot, but major differences in mannerisms and cultures still exist within various geographic regions. We may be a melting pot, but the alloy is not homogeneous, and sometimes the mix seems more the result of alchemy than chemistry. I learned this lesson through the school of hard knocks when I went to college and later entered the business world.

Farm Boy to Fraternity Brother

Growing up on a farm in rural southwestern Ohio did not prepare me for the cultural shock I experienced during my first quarter at The Ohio State University. There were more students in my freshman chemistry class than in the town where I went to high school. The first few days on campus were a total immersion in diversity.

In the dormitory, students were country boys or city slickers, Jews or Christians. On campus, students were out-of-state or in state; foreigners or Americans, blacks or whites, handicapped or able bodied, and so forth. The background diversities of the students I met in classes and when I walked across campus were amazing. I met more types of people in a day than I had my entire life in my small community where everyone was a relative and the term "cuz" for cousin applied to about half of my high school classmates. Although there were differences among the groups, there was no visible animosity: this was the early 1960s - the love generation. For me, however, there was anxiety when I met people from different backgrounds and tried to understand their views. Attending OSU prepared me well for the Midwest, country-boy ribbing and joking that has followed me throughout my life. My Cleveland fraternity brothers, who thought Cleveland was the New York City of Ohio or possibly the center of the known universe, well conditioned me for good-natured verbal abuse. I learned my lesson quickly, and I reciprocated in kind - as I do today when the need arises.

The Midwest Meets the East and the South

After spending seven years on campus, I thought that my social diversification had reached a fairly sophisticated level. This illusion, however, was immediately shattered as I settled into my new job with Campbell Soup Company located in Camden, New Jersey. Even though the company was located in the southern part of New Jersey, it was still very much in the Northeast.

I knew that I was not in Ohio when I was asked primarily by colleagues' wives at social events the baffling question, "Where do your people come from?" I would always answer, "Ohio" and would invariably get a blank stare with a look that said, "I don't believe this guy. He went to college and doesn't even know where his people come from!" It seems obvious now, but what was being asked was where in Europe did my ancestors originate? One's ethnic background was very important in this part of New Jersey, which was still dominated by second and third generation Italians, Polish, and Irish. There was no stigma attached to the origin of one's roots, just an overwhelming curiosity.

I lived in New Jersey for 16 years. Our home was located in a lovely, small village in the middle of vegetable farms (the area that gave New Jersey its Garden State moniker). For some unknown reason, I feel obligated to dispel a few myths about the state. First, there was no Mafia hit guy on every street corner as the TV show The Sopranos would have you believe. Even more important, our neighbors were among the most friendly I had ever met – possibly, something to do with their Quaker heritage. At every level, they were more accepting of newcomers than people in the Midwest and South, where I have lived an equal amount of time.

Being friendly, however, did not stop them from being straightforward, and Campbell Soup Company was the model for straight talk. John McCain named his presidential campaign bus the Straight-talk Express, but straight talk was perfected long ago in the Northeast before the Arizona senator began running for office. You always knew where you stood, and if someone had a problem with your work or you, you knew it. Subtleties, nuances and manners were not used to hide the truth.

Moving from this Northeastern in-your-face communication style to the South where I worked for pre-barbarians-at-the-gates RJR created my next and probably biggest cultural shock. The operating style at RJR was pure southern gentleman, which on the surface sounds great. If you were only visiting, it was a pleasant experience for the non-initiated. If you had, however, been trained in an environment where style points were not given for nuances and subtleties, you were definitely on the outside looking in and out of step with the culture. It took me a couple of months to figure out that even though people were politely smiling when talking with me, they were not necessarily in agreement. Southerners, at least many of those who worked for RJR, did not want to seem rude or unpleasant and preferred to avoid confrontation. It was up to me to figure things out for myself or have someone tell me about my shortcomings. It may seem pleasant from a social perspective to work within this type of environment, but I found it frustrating. Give me your in-the-face communication rather than honey-dripping subtleties anytime. I am not smart enough to read between the lines. Communicating this way slows progress, by distorting reality, and in my view has no place in the workplace. Thank goodness, over time either I have become smarter or this style of communication has become extinct.

You must be polite and diplomatic, but imagine a lawyer who talks in nuances and does not deal with the issues in a straightforward manner. Such a lawyer would be even more exasperating than his or her colleagues, and guidance from such an attorney would be non-actionable. You certainly would not want your medical doctor explaining a diagnosis and treatment in vague terms. When dealing with clients, employees, and suppliers, it is the same for green-industry professionals.

Honest

People cannot call themselves professionals if they are dishonest. A dishonest professional is an oxymoron. When used in the same sentence, the two words are incompatible. Honesty is a 360- degree process for which there is no gap. This is true both in an individual's professional and personal life. Honesty is the cornerstone of integrity. The highest compliments individuals can be paid are that they have high personal integrities. This means they are honest and do what they say they will do.

A RIGHT WAY TO HANDLE DIFFICULT TIMES ---

Sam Lang, the owner of Fairway Green, a lawncare company located in Raleigh, North Carolina, tells a story about a fellow green industry contractor. This contractor owed Sam's company money for subcontracted services - money that was long overdue. The contractor was well known in the Raleigh area and had a good reputation. The economy, however, was creating a major cash flow shortfall for his business, and he was behind in payments to not only Sam, but also many other suppliers. In an effort to save his business and be fair, the contractor sent out a letter to his creditors explaining his financial difficulties, but noting, as well, that his business was sound. He asked them not to press for immediate payment. Doing so, he emphasized, would drive him into bankruptcy, which would result in little money being paid to the people he owed. The financially strapped owner promised his creditors that if they were patient, he would pay everyone in full. A year later, Sam happily reports that all debts were repaid and the contractor survived. The two companies now enjoy a continued, strong working relationship.

SINCERE

Insincere people exhibit a form of dishonesty. They not only cheat the people with whom they are being insincere, they also cheat themselves because they lose value as friends or business associates. Sincere people are genuine in their motives, beliefs, and interactions with other people. Insincerity is a toxic byproduct of envy and jealousy of others - whether it involves personal accomplishments, an individual's station in life, or wealth. Lack of sincerity is easily identified and does not enamor entrepreneurs with their customers and employees.

Landon Reeve, the founder of Maryland-based Chapel Valley Landscape, takes genuine pride when he says that one of the most rewarding aspects of owning a business is seeing his people grow, especially his long-term employees. "They have become successful and so have I," he emphasizes. "Honesty, treating people fairly, and being there to help are very important to developing a loyal staff. So, too, is having a genuine interest in their welfare and trying to understand how you would feel in their shoes." Being sincere defines your character and builds personal equity with every person you meet.

Trustworthy

One could argue that the two terms 'trustworthy' and 'honest' are equivalent, but I consider them different because of an important distinction. A trustworthy person is most likely honest, but the reverse is not necessarily true. An honest person may not always be trusted to stay on task, perform a job, or be punctual. An honest person may lack the skills, training, or motivation needed to be trustworthy. In the broadest of terms, being trustworthy is more important than being honest; trustworthy people do what they say they will do. They can be trusted to follow directions and follow through on promises. In other words you can depend on them. Trustworthiness and honesty are first cousins on the personal-character family tree. These personal characteristics are related, but they have different meanings to me. It is paramount that professionals be both trustworthy and honest. It does not matter how many letters and titles you have behind your name, if you are not trustworthy and honest you are not going to be perceived positively.

The Pay Off

Landon Reeve is a pioneer. When he started his company in the 1960s, there were few landscapers, no real mentors, nor strong local or national professional trade associations. This entrepreneur had no partner with whom he could bounce around ideas and had no friendly banker to fund his new enterprise. Landon said, "I had to fund my business on sweat equity and learn by the seat of my pants." What Landon did have was high personal integrity.

In the early 1970s, when Chapel Valley was still a fairly small residential and commercial landscaping company, Landon became familiar with a general contractor who was building a large corporate headquarters, one of the first in the area. Almost daily for more than three months, Landon reviewed plans with and presented ideas to the contractor. He was so impressed with Landon's perseverance, sincerity, and ideas that he offered the project to Chapel Valley. The estimate for the contract exceeded $300,000, which was a huge project for the young company. This was a career and company-defining moment.

A stumbling block occurred, however, when investors discovered that Landon's company lacked the required bonding, something that was out-of-reach for his small operation. Eventually, the general contractor convinced the investors that Landon was trustworthy and presented him as an honest contractor who should be given a chance. The owners agreed, and the project became one of many that helped Chapel Valley become a major landscape player in the area. "This was a great learning experience," Landon relates. "Never give up no matter how daunting the task may be. Believe in yourself, treat people honestly and sincerely, and good things will happen." It is true more times than not, that one's personal equity is more valuable than money in the bank!

Key to Success

In Chapter II, Hard Work, there is a section on Humility in which I discuss the importance of having a sense of humility when starting a new enterprise or working on a project with others. The same is true when you are in a leadership position - especially when your last name is the same as the 75-year-old company that you are heading. "Humility is the key," responds Dan Ariens, the fourth generation CEO of Ariens Corporation.

> "Many people assume that because you grew up in the business you know everything there is to know about the op-

eration. If you start believing this and walk around the office with a swagger and arrogance, you're bound to make mistakes because no one knows everything about a company as complex as Ariens. Everyone makes mistakes, but if you operate from a platform of ignorant arrogance, you're going to compound the mistakes. To learn, you have to work through the process, experience the hard knocks, and develop your own leadership style. It is a process to develop as a manager because you have to build a leadership profile which is all your own. You have to gain the respect of others, and to accomplish this, you have to respect others. Once this is accomplished, people will be more than willing to follow your directions."

It takes strong personal character, one that is well rooted in self-confidence, to remain humble when a person achieves success or obtains an important position. This is true in both corporate and family-run businesses, but sometimes is even more so in closely held family companies, where some family members may have a sense of entitlement and abuse their positions by arrogant and dictatorial behavior. The professional leaders realize this and lead from positions of humility and engage those around them for input and support.

"You do not lead by hitting people over the head — that's assault, not leadership." — Dwight D. Eisenhower

Service Minded

In my opinion, people cannot be complete professionals unless they are service minded. Webster's defines a professional as, "a person, who, by education, training, and experience, performs work, analyzes and solves problems, makes decisions, and promotes ethics associated with a particular field." When this definition is viewed in a more contemporary light, it is apparent that professionals in today's world are in unique positions to be of service to others. In most cases the highest level of employment of professionals is when they are serving others. Obvious examples are doctors, lawyers and educators, but they do not have a monopoly on caring and sharing. Anyone who has had the opportunity and privilege of reaching the status of being viewed as a professional is in my view, morally obligated to be of service for others.

Here are three excellent examples of role models for service-minded professionals.

THE BUSINESSMAN

Dave Zerfoss, introduced earlier in this chapter, said, "A professional is someone who does not fit in the middle." In other words, professionals are out front as leaders and role models. Professionals have mastered skill sets. True masters have invested 10,000 hours in their craft as reported in ***Outliers*** by Malcolm Gladwell - this is what is needed to become a professional, and you must want to be the best." In Dave's view, professionals are motivated by monetary rewards and status; however, these are not the primary drivers. It is a fire that is fueled by solid core values and a discipline instilled early in life to excel at whatever you choose to do. Dave thinks that there is another important aspect of being a professional that does not get as much focus as it deserves. A complete professional is one who has learned to share both his heart and intellect. This is done even during times when there is not much to share. Paradoxically, it requires a sense of humility to give of oneself to the extent necessary to build a sustainable legacy. From Dave's early farm days to the present, he has mastered the art of being a humble servant.

The Educator

Individuals like Phil Allen, Professor of Landscape Management, Brigham Young University, devote their lives and careers to be of service to others. Business people measure their success in terms of profit and losses, accumulated asset value, and return on investment. In the case of an educator, such as Dr. Allen, success is determined by his or her students - their educations, future vocations, and achieving balanced lives. The passion that drives such a person is a core value - there are no stock options, performance-based bonus, or commission for producing highly educated, trained, and motivated graduates. The success and failure of any industry, and ultimately that of the nation, depends on future generations of professionals and leaders, but there is no financial incentive given for the quantity and quality of students produced - just the reward and love of making a difference in the future of the nation's youth, one student at a time. A natural born educator and volunteer, Phil epitomizes the quote "mankind was my business" (Jacob Marley, *A Christmas Carol* by Charles Dickens).

The Businesswoman

I think that Sharon Barnes, Barnes Nursery, Heron, Ohio sums it up best in her description of a professional as, "Individuals that are passionate about what they do, have uncompromising standards and care for their people and their community, and most importantly measure their successes by these criteria."

Leadership

"Be more concerned with your character than your reputation. Your character is what you really are. Your reputation is what others think you are." – John Wooden

Your personality and character determine what kind of manager and, ultimately, leader you are. To be a successful leader, a person has to have titanium - strong core values that are based on the characteristics that are defined in this chapter and throughout this book.

The 16th Century Italian philosopher and diplomat Niccalo Machiavelli wrote, "It's better to be feared than loved." The implication being that love is a fleeting emotion, but fear is everlasting and is the key to maintaining power over subjects. Simply put, intimidating rulers reign longer than benevolent ones. Machiavelli also observed that the end result usually justifies the means. When I was in college, I had difficulty coming to terms with this ideology. After all, I thought that almost everyone was self-motivated, and leadership should be just a matter of harnessing and directing this motivation.

My beliefs were put to the test when I took my first corporate job. The company I worked for had a strong Machiavellian culture, and leaders subscribed to the hammer-and-anvil approach to managing. The employees, myself included, comprised the anvil. Because I thought I was reasonably self-motivated, I did not appreciate having a hammer over my head and viewed this approach as an archaic throwback. On occasion, I would push back hard; however, when I moved into a supervisor's role and into management, I quickly learned that not everyone is self-motivated. It did not take me long to realize that if I were to be an effective manager and to thrive in the existing corporate culture, I would have to move from a "Mother Teresa" approach to something just short of "Attila-the-Hun" mode of management. Later, when I started my own company, I again found that Machiavelli was right. As an owner, it is easier to lead if you are feared by your employees rather than loved by them. That is not to say that Machiavelli was totally correct because the blatant use of intimidation and fear has the result of driving away some of your best people. Over the years, I have come to the realization that successful entrepreneurial leaders fall somewhere between being feared and being loved by their employees. They are able to obtain the respect of their employees and get their buy-ins without necessarily becoming their best friends. It is a balance and fine art form that has different dynamics with each employee. Professional entrepreneurs figure this out relatively early; otherwise they become as extinct as dinosaurs and australopithecines.

"We herd sheep, we drive cattle, we lead people; lead me, follow me, or get out of my way" – George S. Patton

Fullback to President

John Gibson's first job in the green industry was a mowing crew foreman and his management style was pure Machiavellian - leadership by fear and intimidation. Not that he was a student of the 19th Century Italian prince - his role models were his football coaches in high school and college. After college, he played semi-pro ball, and it was during his time that John mowed during the day, and, by evening, he donned shoulder pads and a helmet to mow down the competition. He was an all–conference, blocking full back and punter who loved to hit and get hit. Sometimes he had trouble separating his day job from the game he loved to play. Once with a smashing forearm shiver after an argument with one of his crewmembers, a he shattered the side window of his company's truck.

Football is a complex, physical sport. The success of the team depends on each player's executing his assignment in a disciplined manner. There is little value in improvising such as is done in basketball and soccer. For success, it is essential that everyone on the team be a team player and bends his will to benefit the team, and the coach is the dictator who makes certain that this happens. At least that was John's experience during his high school and college football days. This was not the case, however, on his semi-pro team. The word "semi" meant the players were not paid and thus were not motivated by money. The coaches, also not being paid, had low-key approaches to the game; so to create the spirit of teamwork motivation had to come from something other than a screaming in-your-face coach. John was more than willing to step to the front and help.

John allows that based on pre-game practice sessions, the coach had a laid-back attitude. The Afro-American players warmed up separately from the rest of the team and practiced a form of self-imposed segregation. Because all the running backs John blocked for were Afro-Americans, he kindly asked the group to join him in practice to iron out some plays. His request was denied.

As a blocking full back, John's primary responsibility was to open holes at the line of scrimmage for the backs to run through. To work properly the timing between a full back and half back has to be precise, and, to be precise, the play has to be practiced over and over. How did John resolve this dilemma? "That was easy," he says. "The first play of the game, I simply stepped aside and allowed the middle linebacker to come rushing through untouched to crush the running back. After that, I no longer had to coax my fellow players to practice as a team."

In sports and business, everyone must be a team player. Your success as a player and as a business operator depends on everyone doing his or her job. Since his football playing days, John's leadership style has mellowed like a premium whiskey aged in an oak cask. He still has plenty of character and is full-bodied, but now he has a deeper understanding of other peoples' feelings, motivations, and perceptions. This has been a formula for success: John is now president of Swingle Lawn, Tree & Landscape Care located in Denver, Colorado. He is many seasons removed from running over linebackers and breaking out truck windows. John credits his success to his boss and mentor - Tom Tolkacz - and to his trade association leadership experience, which helped him develop his management style. John now understands that to be a successful leader he "needs to be in the other person's map of the world." It is less about fear and intimidation and more about being attentive to peoples' feelings, motivations, and perceptions.

"People ask the difference between a leader and a boss. The leader leads, and the boss drives." — Theodore Roosevelt

"My Frame of Mind"

Jennifer Lemcke, the top executive of the Weed Man organization in the United States, achieved her position at a relatively young age. When questioned as to what she thinks her strongest asset is as a leader of a major franchise operation, Jen quickly responded somewhat surprisingly, "My frame of mind." She went on to say that she has a strong sense of positive thinking, a conviction in her abilities, and a work ethic that drives her to win in all situations. She went on to say, "This is my best asset. I always know there is a solution somewhere to be found." To develop her deep and broad experience base, she started at the bottom and worked her way to the top. Along the way, she did every job from finance to human relations, sales to production, and follower to leader at the highest level. She can quickly analyze and cut out the noise and do so with a keen sense of what is right and fair. Her goal when working with others is to achieve a win-win for both parties. She does admit to becoming angry with people who either prevent or stand in the way of a successful solution.

Her leadership style is to focus on building relationships, solving problems, and building something larger than the sum of the parts. She looks to the future with optimism, but, with experienced understanding, she knows that major challenges are always going to occur. She personally likes challenges and being involved in high-level discussions and decisions. Her preferred approach is to be a coach and an instructor, and, as a consequence, she believes her most important impact is through others. One other thing that is apparent when you talk to her is that she loves working with her employees and colleagues. She warns people to not stand too close to her - that what she has may be contagious. This might be a great idea for a franchise!

Landscaper in Paradise

Sometimes, a perfect alignment of time, place, and people occurs, and it changes the course of a person's life and career. The events and factors that come together may be serendipitous, but they are usually not attributable to pure luck. This is especially true for people who work as hard as Robert Hayter. Robert is a Landscape Architect in Pinehurst, North Carolina who became a renaissance professional in the green industry. At a cocktail party, he met a broker who worked for a European business consortium that was planning to build a resort on the Caribbean island of Antigua, West Indies. Robert's insular world of Southeastern landscape design and teaching was knocked out of orbit when the broker asked Robert if he had interest in being the lead landscape architect for the project. Robert expressed interest in pursuing this assignment, and soon found himself sitting across the table from the Prime Minister of Antigua W. I. At the completion of the meeting, the contract was his. As part of the contract, it was agreed that Robert would retain his teaching position with Sandhills Community College and would spend a week out of every month on the site in Antigua.

Most green industry professionals take lifetimes to achieve total accumulative sales of $7 million, let alone achieving such spectacular sales in their first couple of years of operations, but this is what happened when, after the approval of his first contract, Robert started his landscape design and installation business. That is correct - Robert landed a multimillion-dollar landscaping contract and did not have a landscaping business! He had previously dabbled in some entrepreneurial businesses, but his day job was that of an instructor in a technical school. With confidence and a strong character, Robert made a giant leap.

When Robert returned from the Caribbean and announced his good fortune, the President of the College was thrilled that someone from the faculty had gained international attention and brought prestige to the school. This was not, however, the case with the other professors and instructors who protested out of jealousy and envy that this was not fair nor was it in the best interest of the college to have a part-time, globe-trotting instructor on staff. Yielding to peer pressure, Robert made a transcendental decision that changed his career path forever - he resigned his professorship. This turned out to be the right decision, for when he started the planning stages of the project, he quickly realized that because the project was being funded by a consortium of German and Dutch banks, and thus managed from Europe, the traditional operating mode for the lead landscape architect in that environment was simply "You design it - you build it". He was given total responsibility and accountability, an almost unlimited budget, and complete authority over the execution of the work. It was good that Robert was a fast learner and that the many years that he had spent in the academic and business world had prepared him well for this great adventure.

As Robert became submerged in the project, he quickly realized that he could not be a player in the band - he had to be the leader of the band. He learned to delegate and trust his employees, and the results were such a success that Robert was approached by the Italian-designer Krizia Mandelli to design and build the landscape for a private resort on Barbuda, a small island attached to Antigua, W. I. As construction on the first project started winding down, Robert switched his gears to full speed to design and install the landscape for the now-famous K Club Resort in Barbuda. A third project in the Caribbean was also contracted and completed just as the influx of European money funded by Arab oil wealth started to wind down.

Build your character first, and your reputation will follow. This is how Landon Reeve and Robert Hayter built their businesses and careers. In the beginning, there was no impressive picture gallery of completed projects, no award on the wall, nor any referral from a large client. Reeve and Hayter focused on developing their technical expertises and personal characters, and when the times came, they were ready and prepared to take on large complex projects that would have resulted in failures without their previous experience bases. Building and maintaining one's personal character is an ongoing journey that has no final destination or rest stops along the way. One's character must last a lifetime, so there is no short cut or sleeping at the wheel.

I Knew I Had Made it When.....

In my interview of Sharon Barnes, she first surprised me by stating, "I had the grace to come to grips with the past of a very negative experience." Sharon is a successful businesswoman, sits on numerous committees and boards, and is a national composting leader. She helped grow Barnes Nursery to over $10 million in annual sales and headed up one of the largest composting associations in the world. What first came to her mind, however, was the aftermath of surviving a difficult and nasty battle with what she termed "environmental terrorists" who unfairly targeted Barnes and misrepresented facts regarding a marsh that was part of Barnes's private property.

The Army Corps of Engineers had approved an application by Barnes to tap part of the marsh for water for their nursery, but once a local environmental group became aware of the permit, they made life a living hell with false allegations that forced the EPA and the state Attorney General's office into the dispute. Even with experts testifying that there would be no harm, the negative publicity forced the Corps to rescind their approval. After a long drawn out battle, Barnes withdrew their request.

This was a bitter pill, but Sharon admits that she came out stronger and better because of the experience. She indicated that Barnes had taken the high road at all times and held their heads high even though the other side was ignorant and vicious. They navigated the tough times with class and this helped her to define who she is. The experience gave her confidence for the future. "You have to take the horrible experiences in stride knowing that they too will pass, and use them as learning experiences." Sharon knew she had made it when she came through this adversity with her integrity intact. Even though she lost her case, she was able to move on and find other alternatives to fill Barnes' water needs.

"You got to know when to hold 'em, know when to fold 'em." Lyrics from the song The Gambler written by Don Schlitz.

It takes strong personal character and principles to walk away from years of hard work and a large investment of money and time. The lessons that Barnes learned during the water-permit experience were applied again years later when ground that Barnes was leasing for growing nursery stock passed to new owners through inheritance. Even though the heirs were receiving a fair payment of $800 per acre for the land, they figured that they could get more because they thought Barnes would not want to lose the established nursery stock that was growing on the land. The heirs were wrong on two accounts: first they overestimated the rental value of the land, and second they underestimated the resolve of a family that had been in the nursery business for over 50 years. After negotiations went nowhere, Barnes simply bulldozed the stock and returned the land to the heirs. This was a loss for both sides: the heirs' revenue per acre dropped to less than $200 an acre, and the Barnes lost valuable nursery stock. The ultimate winner, however, were Barnes family members who retained their principles and stayed true to their character.

Technician to Business Leader

In Michael E. Gerber's ***EMyth***, which is considered by many to be the "Bible" for entrepreneurs, the thesis is presented that most people who start new businesses have technical expertise about which they are passionate:

- A person who likes to cook starts a restaurant.
- A golf fanatic starts a golf repair shop.

- A baker, who likes to make cakes, opens a sweet shop.
- An individual who loves being outdoors starts a landscaping company.

The common traits are founders all have skill sets they love and falsely think that by starting their own businesses, they will have freedom to follow their dreams of making fabulous wedding cakes or landscape installations. The problem, however, is running an enterprise involves more than just the technical skills. Someone has to sell the products or services, collect revenues, pay bills, and make sure taxes and personnel records are properly managed. In the beginning, the entrepreneur may be able to handle both the craft and business sides of the enterprise, but this is like burning a candle from both ends - soon all that is left are smoke and two burnt ends. This is when tough decisions have to be made. Is the founder going to give up what he or she loves to do (the reason for starting the business), move into the office, start performing administrative functions, or hire help? There is risk of fraud and embezzlement if an outsider is brought in to run the business and maintain the books and handle finances. Many small businesses are ruined by trusted employees who turned out to be dishonest. The other option is to hire crafts people to do the technical work; this deprives the entrepreneur from doing what motivated him or her to start the business. As their business grow, all entrepreneurs must face this dilemma. Some make this transition and others do not. It takes a unique skill set to navigate the path from being a technician to business leader. Robert Hayter puts it succinctly, "At some point you have to quit playing in the band and become the bandleader." Having a strong personal character and a driven desire to accomplish something both help one to succeed in this journey.

It is not, however, just owners who struggle with leadership strategies. One of the most difficult transitions for any person is going from being a worker to becoming a supervisor. When I was in product development at Campbell Soup Company, the standard joke was that when a technician was promoted solely based on technological expertise to a supervisory position, we lost a great technical person and created a poor manager.

Whether it is the move from technical expert to entrepreneur, engineer to project leader, or salesman to regional manager, this step is difficult and involves a quantum leap from one orbit to another with a whole new universe of issues and challenges. Much study and research has been devoted to this subject, and it is similar to the rite of passage discussion that is presented in the Technical Expertise chapter. One of my favorite stories as a young child is the journey of enlightenment of a prince who became king.

The King and the Salt Shaker

> The young king was concerned about the deterioration of his kingdom. There was general unrest in the countryside; people were not paying their taxes, and there were even rumors of rebellion and succession by some of the outlying areas. Worst yet, the peasant farmers were not growing enough food, so the country was facing a food shortage, and there was growing hunger throughout the kingdom. Even the craftsman and merchants were up in arms and reluctant to trade their goods because the value of the currency was so weak. The country was descending into malaise and chaos.
>
> As the king became more isolated from his subjects, following the advice of his military generals and ministers, he deployed troops, who used force. This and the increased taxes to support the troops created more resentment, discontent, and open acts of rebellion - all of which made the king madder and more disappointed. The king's father and grandfather had ruled a peaceful and prosperous country with obedient and loyal citizens, but now it was strife and disobedience. Finally, in desper-

ation, the king approached one of his father's old advisers who had long ago faded into the shadows of bygone days. The wise man did not lecture the young ruler on the ways of the past nor did he point out that the main cause of discontent was the king's arrogant ignorance of his country and people. Instead he gave the king a large royal saltshaker, which he told the king contained magic dust that when sprinkled in the countryside, villages, cities, and throughout the kingdom would resolve the problems. The king at first was dubious, not believing in folklores or magic. He asked how this could be possible and how the powder could have such powers. The old man replied that the situation was desperate, that the king must trust him, and it was imperative that every corner of the empire had to be visited and dusted.

In desperation, but still doubtful, the king immediately set forth. It was a scary adventure for the nobleman - he had never traveled far from the capital and preferred to work through his royal appointments, while he enjoyed the luxuries of his palace. The first couple of days were, at best, tenuous and stifled in that he had a hard time communicating with the villagers and peasants - he did not speak their language. His countrymen were equally uneasy and did not know what to expect - they had not seen a member of the royal family since the king's father had died. The king pressed on, however, and sprinkled magic dust in all the far reaches of his kingdom.

The citizens thought this was unusual behavior, but accepted it as a new royal custom, and it was a lot better than being hounded by tax collectors! A magical thing happened as the king's journey progressed: he learned that his countrymen spoke the same language that he did, but, to understand them, he had to listen to what they had to say. In doing so, he realized that his subjects were good people. The king's journey, which was originally planned for no more than a month, turned into a whole year! So extensive were the king's visits that he had to send the shaker back to the capital numerous times for refills, which the wise old man dutifully but secretly collected from the chalk dust bins of the local school!

"Management by walking around" is stressed in Tom Peters' popular and widely read 1980s book ***In Search of Excellence***, and this is the moral to the story about the king - the best leaders go into the field, meet clients, work shoulder to shoulder with their employees, attend trade-association meetings, benchmark and network with their peers. To be successful you have to be there!

After hearing this story in Sunday school, I tried this approach on my father's farm. I would faithfully walk to every corner of the farm with my magic dust. But nothing seemed to change, we still had weeds, insects, and droughts, but I did get to know the lay of the ground and woods. It wasn't until years later did I truly appreciate the meaning of this allegory. Today when I walked these same fields and woods, I have a vivid recall of what the land looked like then and can easily identify changes that have occurred over the years. So just like Wendy in *Peter Pan*, I too believe in fairy tales and magic dust!

CHAPTER IV

....

Technical Expertise

The Basics

A solid foundation is the most important factor when building a house, a landscape structure, or planting a new lawn. The soundness of the foundation determines the quality and long-term longevity of the building, retaining wall, or turf. The same thing is true for one's career and success in life. A solid foundation of the basics is critical - to be a successful professional, one must be well rounded in English, math, social studies and both physical and biological sciences.

We live in a world of human interaction and communication, and people are quick to make judgments based on how one speaks and writes. Having a fundamental understanding of English is one of the most critical factors defining a professional. With a world population becoming more diverse, the ability to read and speak Spanish is becoming ever more important, especially in the green industry.

Basic math skills are a given - no green industry professional can survive without an ability to work with and understand numbers. Every facet of our industry revolves around numbers - adding, subtracting, multiplying, dividing, and (yes) at times algebra. From work timesheets, to estimate forms, profit and loss statements, material-cost calculations, measurements and formulations, and price lists, numbers are manipulated, plotted, analyzed, reported, and stored. Whether you use a spreadsheet on a computer, a manual calculator, or process the numbers in your head, you have to understand math. If you use spreadsheets, and who does not in this data intensive world we live in, a whole new skill set is required that includes the ability to format, create formulas, link spreadsheets, store and retrieve data. If you graduated before the mid-1980s, you probably did not learn about spreadsheets and computers in school, so if you want to be skilled with his technology, you most likely have had to have been self-taught. Tech-savvy entrepreneurs who embraced this technology early gained advantages over their technically challenged competitors. Successful entrepreneurs realized that being able to analyze vast and complex sets of data would result in faster and more accurate estimates and more precise cost tracking capabilities. This also meant that they did not have to have trained accountants and industrial engineers with calculators, number-two pencils and green-eye shades pounding their numbers - these jobs could be done by people who had basic math skills. The key is that the people have to have fundamental understandings of math because no matter how sophisticated the spreadsheet programs or how powerful the computers, if the people doing the work do not have basic understandings of math principles, there is no advantage, and the added expense of the technology is wasted. It is like having a supersonic jet at one's disposal but only having a single-engine pilot's license.

The next element of one's foundation is a working knowledge of both physical and biological sciences. This does not mean that one has to be a scientist, but one does need to know basic principles. Our world is wondrous, and anyone making a living in the green industry should have a basic understanding of the life forces at work. One of the key life forces is photosynthesis. This process fuels all living beings, and without it there would be no life, and earth would be one, giant desolate rock orbiting the sun. All our food, fiber and much of our energy come from the miracle of converting carbon dioxide, moisture, and sunshine into complex carbon structures. If not for plants, there would no animal life. Photosynthesis is the only living process that creates and stores energy - all other aspects of life consume it. Energy comes from sunlight, which plants capture and convert into energy stores that sustain all of our planet's animal life. Because of the earth's ideal location in the solar system, we have the perfect environment for human life. A slightly different location and this beautiful planet would be nothing but desert or ice. In addition, our proximity to the moon creates tidal currents that sustain much of our flora and fauna. Knowing and understanding these processes, helps us appreciate what a special gift we have and how important it is to protect the finite resources we have here on earth.

To be successful in the green industry, it is also critical for you to understand plant physiology and the dynamics of agronomy. Without this fundamental knowledge, it is difficult or impossible to care for complex plants. In the green industry, the key today is sustainability. Understanding and having an appreciation for the life forces at work helps us design and maintain sustainable landscapes for our children and us. The word "sustainability" has equal relevance in the business world. Without having a fundamental-knowledge base, it is difficult to survive in an increasingly competitive marketplace.

The Rite of Passage - Initiation, Internship, Apprenticeship

Over the last two centuries, the training and education in crafts, trades, and professions has evolved from a master-apprenticeship relationship to technical schools, colleges, and universities. In the U.S. from the 1970s through the 1980s, emphasis was placed on everyone going to college and receiving a liberal arts education. Technical education at the college level was considered vocational, and, at the time, the common wisdom of our education and national-decision makers was that a liberal arts education better prepared people for white-collar careers that would be created and would balance the expected loss of blue-collar jobs in the manufacturing sector. Europe, with its long tradition of trade guilds (masons, printers, tanners, and textile workers), did not jump on the liberal arts education bandwagon. This was also true for Asian powerhouses - such as Japan and South Korea. This is not to say that the rest of the world did not place an emphasis/premium on liberal arts education - Cambridge, Oxford and Heidelberg Universities focus on this kind of education. In these other countries, however, only those students with the highest test scores and proficiencies were granted entrance into the elite schools. For many students, their future careers were determined in high school by their successes or failures in a series of attribute tests. The U.S. followed the democratic tradition and through community, state, and private institutions provided almost everyone with an opportunity to obtain an education after high school. The rest of the world was focusing their educational resources on training the majority of their young people in technical and vocational subjects.

I know it is hard to argue against the success of the American system of universal education; we boast of many of the top schools in the world, and we have one of the highest standard of living rankings. There are, however, some glaring weaknesses - low math and science scores, high dropout rates, and large numbers of graduates who are ill prepared for any kind of work. With that said, I think that we in the U.S. should be concerned. Based on the experiences I have had and observations I made during my corporate days when I traveled around the world as a process and product developer, I learned (and I find it hard to admit) that the European and Asian manufacturers had superior engineering and manufacturing capability. Italy was by far the best fabricator of stainless steel food processing equipment. The Italians, along with the Germans, were, and still are, leaders in manufacturing and precision assembling. Excellent examples here include Ferrari, Maseratti, BMW, and Porsche. The English are also very good at high-end equipment manufacturing - Rolls-Royce cars and jet engines. The Japanese Toyota company is now the largest and most respected car manufacturer in the world, and Sony has long led the world in electronic products.

The English, being English, had and still do have, to the best of my knowledge, a provincial view of engineering/technical endeavors. Any occupation that requires working with one's hands is considered a low-class occupation. It is much more prestigious and socially acceptable for people to work in the industries of banking and financial ventures. When questioned on this distinction, the stock answer was, "Well, old chap, that is where the money is." Another English trait is that they have some of the best research and science institutions in the world, but they have a relatively poor record of transitioning their innovations into widely used products. I guess it is because they do not want to get their hands "dirty" or are afraid of pursuing careers in which they would never be invited to have tea with the Queen!

Since WW II, this has not been a problem for the Japanese. They are the world's masters (with the Chinese closing fast) at capitalizing on their technology or anybody else's for that matter. They seem to consider that their biggest successes are those that result from their begging, borrowing, or stealing ideas and technology. The ultimate success is when they are given an idea/technology for free! For years, the Swiss were known as the best watchmakers in the world, and this was without question in the 1970s. Swiss clock makers had mastered the fine art of engineering precision gears and jeweled movements. This craft was perfected after centuries of continuous advancements in every aspect of clock production. This experience base, coupled with the Swiss's world marketing dominance for fine time-keeping devices created a feeling of arrogance and having myopic vision regarding their view of the future and their competitors' abilities. They were so confident and convinced that the market would always demand the craftsmanship of a mechanical wristwatch that when their own R&D department developed and demonstrated an electronic quartz watch, management dismissed this innovation as a novelty and a cheap antithesis of a handcrafted analog watch. When the rebuffed R&D engineers asked if they could exhibit their development at an upcoming international tradeshow, permission was given, and watch history was changed forever. Visiting the tradeshow was a contingent of Japanese engineers -

they liked what they saw and, within 10 years, the wristwatch industry was revolutionized. The world capital of watch making moved from Geneva to Tokyo - thanks to a development that was invented in a lab in Switzerland and figuratively handed to the Japanese on a silver platter - a gift that keeps on giving. It is one thing to be so blind as to not anticipate the threat of new technology to your product line or business, but it is quite another thing for you to develop the technology and give it away! The resulting paradigm shift is not what is strived for by business people.

It is worth considering "Whether the American downturn in manufacturing, especially at the high-end level, is due to cheap labor in other countries or due to not having highly-trained, vocationally-skilled journeymen." It is, of course, a combination of both factors, but I argue that the later is the dominant reason.

APPRENTICESHIP

Today, colleges and universities have taken the place of the traditional apprenticeship. Long gone are the days when an aspiring lawyer or craftsman worked and learned in servitude to a master. This would be too clumsy in today's world and not enough people could be trained or educated to meet the demands of a modern society. Elements of the old system of apprentices and interns, however, still remain. When I was in graduate school, one of the favorite sayings was that being a graduate student was the last legalized form of slavery. I am sure the medical interns thought the same thing, and if the popular medic TV shows are remotely accurate to true life, this is still the case today. The similarities are striking - student = slave; master = faculty advisor. The apprenticeship begins with your advisor helping to select your coursework, determine your research and ultimately is the master of your destiny - if he/she does not sign/approve your thesis/dissertation, you do not graduate. At the master's level, when the coursework is completed and the research thesis is written, it is time to go before a faculty committee to defend your work. The committee determines whether or not you are worthy of being admitted into the "advanced degree club." Admittance at this junior level (masters) is not as jealously guarded as is the Ph.D. inner circle, but there is a price to pay, and an initiation ritual through which you must go. I am thankful that as the time approached for me to defend my thesis, a doctorarial student from Australia named Jeff Fairbrother asked me if I was prepared for my big exam. I quickly replied, "Jeff, I know my subject up and down and sideways; no one knows more about my research project than I do." Jeff looked at me with an easy smile that all Australians seem to possess and said, "That's not what I asked. What I asked, are you prepared for the 'walk about' all graduate students must go through if they want to pass their committees and get their degrees." He went on to explain that you must show respect and be deferential and miss, at the least, one or two questions. I immediately responded, "There is not one question regarding my subject this group can ask me that I do not know." Jeff's smile faded as he said, "Mate, you are totally missing the point. Getting your masters degree is the key to allow you into their elite club, so if you do not miss a question or say that you do not know the answer, they are not going to allow you to graduate." The simple reason is because they have to maintain their sense of superiority. I heard what Jeff said, but I dismissed his advice as being from someone who came from the country down under and had blood rushing to his head as he grew up in the Southern Hemisphere. On the day of my defense, I went into the committee exam room loaded for bear. After an exchange of pleasantries, the questions started and my confidence grew with every question as I smashed each out of the ballpark. After about 30 to 40 minutes, the atmosphere began to change, and the questions became sharper; smiles turned into locked jaws; the committee members' eyes narrowed; and the atmosphere turned into one of an inquisition. The only thing missing was a bright spotlight. It finally dawned on me that they were not going to let me out of the room until I admitted that I did not know all the answers to their questions. This I did, and within five minutes the defense was over. I passed and being a little wiser, lived to go through a similar ritual two years later - when I did the walkabout during my two-hour defense of my Ph.D. thesis.

Zerfoss and the Zen of Motor Repair

Where there is a will, there always seems to be a way to make the things happen that you want to happen. Dave Zerfoss's parents had no money for Dave to go to college, but they could provide room and board in exchange for help on the farm, so Dave enrolled at the local college, Indiana University of Pennsylvania. While at school, he carried a full course load, worked 50 to 60 hours per week, and managed to graduate in four years. He was a liberal arts major with a focus on economics. His studies in finance and economics gave him a solid footing for his career. During this period, not all of Dave's education was taking place in the classroom. One of his part-time jobs was working in a foreign-car repair shop where he worked alongside a master technician who taught Dave the art of mechanics. This is where Zerfoss learned to break a system down into its components, analyze the system, make distinctions, and reassemble the parts to make a better whole. Nothing forces your attention more than tearing down a 12-cylinder Jaguar motor, cleaning each part, repairing and replacing defective pieces, and re-assembling the engine into a smooth-running, high-powered machine. Dave may have been taking liberal arts courses, but his part-time jobs were the laboratories where he began learning the mastery skills he needed for a successful business career. Working with your hands in a car repair shop may seem like an odd place to learn technical and analytical skills; however, considering that this was the norm for craftsmen and business people just a couple of generations ago, this is not so unusual. Perhaps a return to this type of apprentice system might help America regain its prominence in manufacturing and technology.

"Horticulturists Don't Know Nothing!" Tak Ishida

When Bill Arman graduated with an ornamental horticulture degree from Cal Poly, his first job was with Green Valley Landscapes, which later became known as ValleyCrest - today one of the largest integrated landscape companies in the U.S. Upon meeting Bill, his new boss, Mr. Tak Ishida, exclaimed in a loud voice to the recent horticulture graduate, "Ha, ha. Horticulturists don't know nothing!" So with this drill-sergeant style of orientation, Bill began his apprenticeship under the master, Mr. Ishida. Tak was a five-foot-four inch, samurai-style disciplinarian, who believed in hard work and the basics. Bill started at the bottom of the labor pool with a backpack blower and followed the Hispanic mowing crews to disperse clumps of glass clippings. He realized immediately that if he were going to be accepted, he would have to work as hard as his fellow team members, and this would be not be easy in that he would have to work his tail off every day. Mr. Ishida, impressed by Bill's efforts, overcame his bias against horticulturists and adopted Arman by taking him under his wing. Once accepted by the boss, the other team members quickly came over to his side and respectively referred to him as their "great white hope."

Mr. Ishida was a California-born strawberry farmer, so he had deep roots in agriculture, and an affinity with nature that only someone who has worked with soil all his life possesses. Tak was so impressed that a college guy had such a strong work ethic for the outdoors and a passion for plants that he arranged their schedules so that he and Bill could meet on coffee breaks to discuss work and life in general. Like the cultivation of a bonsai plant, a slow and gentle process of shaping and forming, Tak helped Arman shape his vision for the future and set him on the right path for a lifetime. This act of kindness was based on respect and a desire to share one's talents with another being. Over the years, Bill has paid back Ishida's gift by sharing his knowledge and experience with many of those with whom he comes in contact. After 30-plus years in the corporate landscape world, Bill is now a managing partner in a well-respected green industry consulting group and continues to cultivate the potentials of others.

Technical Expert - Drip Under Pressure

A graduate school student is an apprentice at two levels (student and researcher) plus, if you are also a teaching assistant, there is the added level of being an employee. One day when I was teaching a lab class on how to conduct a tin can, top-seam analysis, the head of the department (my boss) walked into the room. The class of approximately 20 students, 19 to 21-year-old males, immediately came to attention. Dr. Wilbur A. Gould was both loved and feared by undergraduates (graduate students mostly feared him); he was friendly and gave entertaining lectures, but was also a stern disciplinarian. This day he was in rare form. He started by saying hello to the class and stating, in an authoritative voice, that this class was one of the more important labs that students take. He went on to say that if the top seam of the can leaked during the retort sterilization process the food could be contaminated by a bacterial toxin, and, in rare cases, this could cause people to die. He emphasized that everyone should pay special attention to Dr. Hildebolt, for "he is an expert on this subject." Correcting himself he said, "Oh, did I say Doctor? " With wink of his eye, he continued, "Bill may tell you that he is getting a doctorate, but he hasn't gotten it yet." With a huge smile on his face, he turned on his heel and walked from the classroom. As the door closed, I tried to regain composure, but no more than 15 seconds later, as I was in mid-sentence, the door reopened, Dr. Gould stuck in his head and said, "By the way, do you know what the definition of an expert is? Well, my definition is, it is a drip under pressure!"

Rites of passage and initiations are common within our culture - be they social, family, educational, business, military, religious, secret society, or sports team.

- Fraternities/sororities - pledges to brother/sister
- Professional sports teams – rookies to veterans
- Academic institutions–instructor, assistant professor, associate professor, full professor
- Military - private to general
- Business - trainee to CEO
- Family - baby, child, teenager, young adult, parent, grandparent, senior citizen, patriarch/matriarch

It is important to remember that any time you enter into an organization as a newcomer, there will be a time of adjustment for you to become familiar with the other people and they with you. This process cannot be circumvented; the military and gangs mark this process as "earning your stripes". This behavior pattern is not limited to human beings, as I learned growing up on my father's farm. We had a hog production operation, and when the baby pigs reached about 30 pounds in weight, it was time for them to be weaned from their mothers. At this point, each litter of six to eight piglets was combined with about 10 other litters and placed in a large feeding area. This was where it got scary. Even though the pigs had the same father and were born and raised in pens next to each other, when they were released together, it was all-out war with each litter fighting with every other litter. They would fight to the death, no matter how hard we tried to separate them. The only solution was to spray the pigs with diesel fuel to mask the unique odor of each litter. When I questioned my dad and grandfather about this, they said that pigs were territorial and instinctively attacked any other pig that was not of their litter. I have often wondered if humans also carry this genetic disposition!

Connections

Technical expertise has always been an important driver in human development. Major milestones in civilizations are referred to as the Stone,

Bronze, Iron, and Industrial ages. Cultures with the most advanced technology defeated and surged ahead of their less sophisticated neighbors. Some of the advancements were seemingly simple refinements of what existed, but these refinements gave their innovators competitive advantages - which happened with the addition of a stirrup to the saddle and the development of the shoulder harness. With the foot stirrup, riders can accurately thrust a sword or spear from the back of a horse. This is a huge advantage over foot soldiers and other riders without stirrups. The stirrup originated in China about 100 A.D., and, approximately 700 years later, it was the basis for the evolution of the Europe's feudal system during which knights on horses enforced the rules of the land as defined by the overlords. Equally important, when the horse was the only major source of power, was the adaptation of the harness, which transfers the weight of object being pulled to the horse's shoulders. The previous approach was to use a noose around the horse's neck, but, as the horse pulled harder, the noose tightened and the horse was strangled. By transferring the weight to the horse's shoulders, for the first time plows could be pulled, which vastly increased the amount of ground that could be cultivated in Europe. As a result, tribes that had previously depended mostly upon hunting and gathering formed permanent agriculture communities with a concomitant increase in the population of Europe.

Crusaders mounted on horses with armored plating were, however, no match for gunpowder and muskets that began appearing in Europe in the 16th Century. The Chinese invented gunpowder during the Tang Dynasty (8th Century) when they discovered that heating a mixture of sulfur and saltpeter with charcoal produced a powerful explosive. The enterprising Chinese later found that filling bamboo tubes with gunpowder could launch arrows - in time this discovery would lead to the rocket launcher and rifle. When the conquistadors adapted both the horse and gun power to their military prowess, they became devastating conquerors of the New World.

Other advancements have had profound influences on the advancement of knowledge and travel. In 1448, a German named Johannes

Gutenberg invented the printing press, which for the first time allowed mass production of books and pamphlets that had enormous impacts on the dissemination of information. A little over 300 years later, Thomas Paine's ***Common Sense*** pamphlet was credited with being one of the major factors in convincing neutral colonialists to join the revolutionary forces of George Washington. The Industrial Revolution was ushered in 1769 when James Watt, a Scotsman, patented the modern steam engine. Less than 30 years later, John French obtained a U.S. patent for a steamboat, and later Robert Fulton pioneered steam navigation. In 1843, the launching of the iron-hulled, propeller-driven steamship, SS Great Britain, started an inter-continental shipping race. The propellers that drove these ships were adaptations of the Archimedes screw that was invented in the 3rd Century BC, during the time that the first Roman sundial was perfected and the Hopewell Culture in Ohio appeared - a connection that spanned over two millenniums. The propeller eventually lead to the demise of sailing ships, and in the latter part of the 1800s the steam locomotive became one of the main drivers in opening the western territories of the U.S.

With the coming of the 20th Century, the rate of technological advancement accelerated. The internal-combustion engine began replacing steam engines and horses and buggies were turned into horseless carriages, wagons to trucks, and steam locomotives to diesel powered trains. In 1903, the Wright brothers flew the first airplane. Alexander Bell's telephone, Thomas Edison's phonograph, and Guglielmo Marconi's radio (all patented many years previously) began to be widely used. People were befuddled and amazed that the human voice could be captured in wax or transmitted over the airwaves and played back through a speaker in a box! For people who did not have electricity nor running water, traveling at over 60 miles an hour in a passenger train or flying like a bird were incomprehensible miracles.

Today we accept radio, TV, cell phones, satellite GPS receivers, and computers with wireless Internet service as necessities and rites of our modern lives, but a mere 100 years ago, the much-simpler technologies discussed in the previous paragraph baffled and amazed our grandparents and great-grandparents. Even as ubiquitous as the car has become, the first horseless carriages were frightening and confusing mechanical monsters. My grandfather delighted in telling the story of a relative who having succeeded in getting his new Model T into forward gear could not figure out how to stop it. In frustration and fear, he desperately kept yanking back on the steering wheel and shouting "Whoa!" until the car ran into a tree! This reminds me of when I learned to operate my first computer: I cursed at it and shut it off - before the temptation to throw it across the room became irresistible.

The purpose of this brief and exceedingly narrow history of the evolution of technology and the advancement of technical expertise is to illustrate that almost every innovation is actually the adaptation of previous knowledge and experience. For further reading on this subject, I suggest James Burke, a British scientist and historian who has published extensively on invention and discovery; Burke is best known for his British Broadcasting Corporation documentary series entitled "Connections" during which he tracks technology and its impact on history. It provides strong reinforcement for making connections (networking and benchmarking within your chosen profession).

Spinning Yarn to Chain Saws

One of my favorite connection stories includes the spinning wheel, a circular saw blade and a Shaker spinster (no pun intended) by the name of Tabitha Babbit. In 1813, Miss Babbit observed the inefficiency of two men cutting a log in a saw pit and came up with the idea of putting teeth on a circular blade patterned after her spinning wheel. This stroke of insight became the first mechanized circular blade used in a sawmill, and, when connected to a water wheel and later to a steam engine, the lumber and wood working crafts were forever changed. Today the legacies of this ingenious mind are hand-held, electrical circular saws and two-cycle engine chainsaws. If Tabitha had not had experience spinning woolen yarn with a spinning wheel when she observed the back-and-forth motion of a draw saw, she would not have visualized a circular saw blade to cut wood. One has to be there, observe, and make connections. Just like James Watt saw the lid rattle on his mother's boiling kettle and visualized steam power, Tabitha Babbit saw her spinning wheel and visualized woodchips.

Mass Force Replaced by Knowledge Based Power

Over the centuries human hierarchal power has primarily evolved from positions of strength, religious beliefs, gender, and inheritance. The strongest and most aggressive tribes subjugated their neighbors and the surrounding regions. The strongest warriors became the leaders of their clans and were assisted by their shamans who supported their leaders through teaching of myths and superstitions. As time passed, traditions became canons and laws whereby the power structure was maintained for those in control and was passed down to their heirs. In Europe, this process developed into a monarchial system that was dominated by the royalty who controlled the land and the people through brutal force. This was not, however, unique to Europe: Russia had its czars and serfs, Asia its emperors and peasants, and the Aztecs their chiefs and slaves. As a way to help people understand their places and roles in society, religion was dispersed to all of these cultures. For keeping masses of uneducated people in line, the power of faith in a belief system is much stronger than knights mounted on horses or any other type of police force. This was well understood by the mainly male leaders of the time - people who could not be conquered by physical power could be manipulated by superstition and the promise of bliss in the afterlife. During the last 200 years, there have been numerous godlike earthbound leaders in Europe, South America, and Asia. North America has also had its share of demigods, most recently in the form of Jim Jones and David Koresh.

"DOWNSIDE UP AND UPSIDE DOWN"

Until recently, hierarchal structures evolved slowly; in many parts of the world, centuries-old belief structures are still in place - maybe not as dominant as they once were but their vestiges still linger. The czars are gone, but the serf mentality of post communist Russia is still pervasive in much of the country. The Chinese replaced their emperors for a demagogue by the name of Mao Zedong, and even after the great communist Cultural Revolution, peasants still outnumber city dwellers. In many parts of the world, however, with continual quantum jumps in the advancement of technology and the dissemination of knowledge, traditional hierarchal structures are coming under attack like no other time in history. This is happening at such a rapid pace that a paradigm shift may occur within the next 10 to 15 years - with systems that we now recognize being upside down and inside out. It has already started in some places. The Millennials who are following the Generation X and Baby Boomers are leading this revolution by their complete acceptance and fluency with everything electronic, digital logic, and virtual intelligence. Like no previous generation, they have incorporated the latest devices and technology into their being and characters. They are the drivers and the driven of this high-tech explosion, which is figuratively as powerful as was TNT in the 19th Century and nuclear fusion in the 20th Century. The Millennials are digital beings. There is a tsunami-like force that is building and is about to hit all organizational structures in virtually every country in the world. The survivors will be those who control the technology, and they will assume the new leadership positions. Those who are currently on top will be replaced by their more tech-savvy colleagues. Age, experience, and pedigree will become second level considerations for promotions to management and decision-making positions. Knowledge is power and instantaneous knowledge will belong to those who control the technology. To glimpse into the future, all you have to do is look at how Google has blown past GE and Microsoft in net worth and influence in a mere 10 years. The organization chart is going to be reversed with the youngest and least tenured employers at the top of the pyramid and the senior employees at the base. Those who were in are now going to be out. This change is going to happen faster than anyone over 30 can imagine. As Glenn H. Tecker, Tecker Consultants, LLC, described in a 2009 management symposium, for most of us, this experience will be strangely like sitting around the campfire several millenniums ago with the tribal elders asking their children, "Now tell us again, how you invented this thing called fire?" For people in hierarchal structures, they are going to feel like a twisted sock turned inside out.

"Don't you just want to twist and shout when you are outside in?"
Lyrics from the song Inside Out by The Traveling Wilburys.

I like to try to imagine what questions elders around campfires will be asking the new generation approximately 20 years from now when my grandchildren will be graduating from college. My hope is that there will be a real fire under a moonlit sky, with face-to-face discussions and not virtual individuals who are being produced by the latest electronic devices.

Change at the Speed of Light

It is important to understand that these trends are coming and are coming figuratively at the speed of light. You need to begin adapting now. Not only are your employees going to be changing, they are also going to be challenging you, and concomitantly customer expectations are going to change. The competitive landscape will be a dynamic battlefront. The advantage will no longer be to those with the largest budgets and staffs. Small entrepreneurial companies will have the same computer horsepower as much larger bureaucratic organizations and will be much quicker to adapt and make changes as new technology evolves. New organizations will have a distinct competitive advantage, because they will be willing to hire the young techs and put them in positions to drive change. The entrenched traditional businesses are going to be reluctant to make these moves because of vested interests of the top management. Some positions may become obsolete - these include infield sales forces of landscapers and lawncare companies. Estimates and proposals will be based on satellite imaging and done in real time over the telephone and Internet. GPS route scheduling and in-truck invoicing is already here, and this may eliminate existing middle management positions. The playing field is becoming flatter each year. In the near future its flatness will be virtual.

When an era changes, you either adapt or go extinct. In the past, this was a gradual process, which sometimes took centuries. There was time to adapt to changes - just like a glacier passing over rough terrain, leveling and pulverizing everything in its path. Once the glacier melts away, the landscape is changed forever. The plants and habitat that survive had time to adapt to their new environment. Such was the case of the Wisconsin Glacier that, 20,000 years ago, turned the U.S. Midwest into the most productive agricultural land and diverse habitat for plants and wildlife in the world. The massive weight of the glacier ground the rock into fine powder that became the building blocks for the fertile black topsoil that is now the breadbasket of the world.

Over the last two centuries, the half-life of technical change for each subsequent era has decreased. Today, during a person's lifetime, multiple technological eras occur. Computer speeds continue to increase and their costs continue to go down. At times, these rapid changes may seem to be overwhelming for some peoples' minds and spirits. *Homo sapiens* are, however, an adaptable species that evolved in Africa and are able to populate and thrive in all regions of the world. Other species are not so fortunate with tens of thousands of species becoming extinct each year. The ones that adapt survive; they embrace changes, develop competitive advantages, and thrive. This is what professionals do - they know that change is a constant, and like captains at sea, they watch the horizons for opportunities and dangers. They know when to sail full speed ahead and when to take cover from gathering storms or stand and fight off pirates. They neither fear change nor blindly chase after promises of sunny skies. They stay up to date and maintain their technical expertise, which requires constant attention. Mastery of one's craft and industry does not ensure permanent professional security or business dominance, as is illustrated by the history of the shipping industry.

Centuries of Domination to Obscurity in One Generation

Sailing vessels from the time of the Vikings, Christopher Columbus, and Magellan through the mid-19th Century, were the dominant means of sea travel. Sailing ships had a Gordian-Knot monopoly; there was no other form of transportation for war or peace that could rival them - until the invention of the steam engine by James Watt and the iron-hulled, propeller-driven steam ship. The race was on as to who would build the fastest and the largest ocean liner. The sailing ship builders rose to the occasion by designing boats with ever-larger sails and redesigned hulls to gain as much speed as possible. Large sails, however, require large crews to raise and lower them and cause the ships to be top heavy. So from a practicality standpoint, there is a limit on how much sail can be mounted on a sailing vessel. For steam powered ocean liners, there was no such restriction. The only limiting factor was the amount of fuel that could be carried, but because coal and cordwood were plentiful and could be purchased in almost any port throughout the world, this was a minor limitation. In addition, a propeller driven ship could sail in all kinds of weather, with little regard to whether or not the wind blew. Within a relatively short period, the sailing skills of captain and crews became obsolete as were sheets (ropes) and sails, and master shipbuilders had to look for employment elsewhere. Just as Alexander the Great solved the puzzle of the Gordian Knot by cutting it in two, the steam engine cut the sails from the future of ocean liners. Sailing ships governed the high seas for centuries and were replaced in less than a half a century because of the phenomenon that when water is heated to 212°F, it changes phase to steam that can push a cylinder connected to a crankcase to turn a propeller.

"The King Is Dead, Long Live the King"

The steam engine became king in a relatively short time, but almost as soon as it became king, a new technology was on the horizon - the internal combustion engine. Those who owed their fortunes to steam power put all their resources and energy into making a steam engine that had the mobility and fuel efficiency of the internal combustion engine. The Baldwin Locomotive Works, the premier steam locomotive builder from the Civil War up through World War II, feverishly tried to improve the efficiency of the steam engine while ignoring the obvious advantages of diesel power. They stopped building locomotives in 1956 and went bankrupt in 1972. Although the internal combustion engine continues to be used in cars, trucks and ships, it has been replaced by the jet engine in large aircraft. No matter how advanced a technology, nor how educated and trained one is in producing the technology, no technology has proven to be irreplaceable. To have continued success, it is critical for professional entrepreneurs to never stop learning and adapting to change. The world's best buggy-whip maker's success was short lived once Henry Ford started mass-producing Model Ts. No matter how hard the buggy-whip maker worked, nor how wonderful the whips, there was no demand for a product that had been essential in a by-gone era.

Innovators

"The innovator has for enemies all who have done well under the old, and lukewarm defender in those who may do well under the new." Machiavelli

Henry Ford was a visionary who was not satisfied with the status quo. He was a member of a rare breed of innovative entrepreneurs who fulfill their dreams by inventing, developing, modifying, and/or borrowing from other industries. That is, they develop their expertise to fulfill their visions. These individuals change the course of their industries and, in some cases, create entirely new business models. Examples are John Deere and the moldboard plow; the Wright brothers and the flying machine; Bill Gates and Microsoft software; and Steve Jobs and the iPhone.

The same is true for individuals and enterprises. If you are not continuously reinventing your business model and reinvesting in your own technical skills, then someone else will. Most innovations come from outside an established industry. Just like the Swiss watch manufacturer who dismissed the development of the quartz watch by their own R&D department, many established businesses reject innovations made by outsiders out of arrogance and ignorance. Following are two recent innovations that turned their respective industries upside down, and were accomplished by entrepreneurs with no industrial experience in the products they developed.

Dyson Vacuum Cleaner

A British inventor by the name of James Dyson, frustrated by the inefficiency of the household vacuum cleaner, employed his industrial cyclone dust capturing experience to develop the first bag-less vacuum cleaner. He built over 1,000 prototypes before he finally perfected what is now the most powerful and one of the top-selling vacuum cleaners in the world. He offered his invention to major manufacturers but was turned down by all. They were invested in the old technology and were too addicted to selling the replacement bags to clearly see the future. Or maybe they could not see for the dust in the air from their soon-to-be obsolete design.

SawStop Table Saw

Steve Gass, Ph.D., an amateur woodworker who recognized the danger of a table saw, was appalled at the numerous finger and hand injuries that occurred using this piece of equipment. He envisioned a system that would stop a saw blade immediately on touching human flesh. He successfully built a prototype that constantly monitored the conductivity of the saw blade as it cut through wood. If the microprocessor sensed a deviation in current that occurs if the blade comes in contact with a finger, an aluminum blank is instantly thrust into the rotating blade and the drive motor is turned off. Dr. Gass took his prototype to a tradeshow and demonstrated this innovative safety feature using hot dogs. The response from the attendees to make this technology available was so positive, Steve and two partners founded the company SawStop to license his development to table saw manufactures. The story was the same as Dyson's - no manufacturers were interested. They viewed this innovation as a costly add-on and a possible legal liability issue. Rejected, but not dissuaded, the three founders then determined that SawStop would manufacture the best and most technically advanced table saw on the market using Dr Gass's safety innovation. This was in 2004 and today the combined benefits of safety and top-of-the-line craftsmanship have resulted in SawStop being the number one selling cabinet saw.

Dyson and Gass are my kind of innovators. I bought a SawStop table saw for my wood shop two years ago, and it is the safest and best-engineered tool that I own. Sandi, my wife, loves her Dyson vacuum cleaner so much she will not even allow me to use it, even if I volunteer to help clean the house. Both inventors saw a problem, developed the solution, and when no one would adapt their innovation, they went out on their own and developed products that in a relatively short number of years, now dominate the industries that originally rejected them. They are excellent models for 21st Century professional entrepreneurs – propreneurs - in the truest sense.

Both Dyson and Gass were victims of "NIH" syndrome – Not Invented Here. For those familiar with creativity tools and techniques, this is a well-known block to creativity and innovation. The NIH syndrome is a first cousin to "killer phrases" - words used by those with a vested interest in the status quo or who simply don't understand the importance of new ideas. Examples of killer phrases include: "We tried that before; That won't work here; If it ain't broke, don't fix it; Yes, but...; That'll never fly; Put it in writing; and The boss will never go for it." If you have ever been guilty of using words like these when presented with something new or different, here is a great tool to overcome this trap – "PIN." PIN stands for Positive, Interesting, and Negative. First, you must say something Positive about the idea before proceeding. Next, say something Interesting about the idea. Last, you can talk about why you don't think it is a good idea (Negative). An important corollary to use at this point is to brainstorm ways to overcome the Negative. If you find yourself on the receiving end of a killer phrase or the victim of NIH, remember Dyson and Gass and don't give up. Often times, the person who hit you with the killer phrase will be more receptive after he has had time to consider your idea, even if only subconsciously. For those who would like more on creativity and innovation, read ***The 7 Levels of Change*** by Rolf Smith.

It is important to understand in one's personal and business concerns there is a human behavior tendency to reject new ideas or suggestions when they are presented for the first time. Early in my career as a research technologist, I would eagerly go to my boss with what I thought was a great idea only to be dismayed that he did not enthusiastically support my proposal. Since, I was in product development this became a regular routine and after a while I became less sensitive to what I perceive as rejection from my boss. Eventually, I began to see a pattern developing in that after a couple weeks of making a suggestion, my boss would ask about the status or progress of the proposal. This did not happen on all of my ideas, but on enough of them that it got my attention. At first I was surprised he had remembered our conversation, and secondly embarrassed to inform him, "Not a damn thing!" Not receiving an initial positive response, I had moved on to my next 'great idea'. After this occurred several times, the light bulb finally went on, and I change my tactics. I eventually figured out the best way to get buy-in for a new idea was to do the 'ground work' ahead of time. Just like a gardener prepares the soil before planting a crop I would drop little hints and suggestions before sowing the seeds of a new concept. This would involve asking for my boss's input and participation by trying to capture his imagination so he would share the vision and ownership of the proposal. Once I perfected this approach, it worked on every boss I ever had. It is not magic to get acceptance of your ideas - it is simply understanding human nature.

One other important lesson I learned as a student and employee is that individuals in responsible positions, whether they are educators or business people, will always come to your aid if you simply ask for their help.

BEST IN CLASS

In the green industry, one of the best examples of a pioneer who literally changed the landscaping world is Burt Sperber. In the 1950s, when Burt started ValleyCrest, the commercial and residential landscape and nursery businesses were primarily operated as stepchildren to big brother agriculture. Equipment manufacturers were singularly focused on high-volume crops such as fruits and vegetables in California, and corn, soybeans, and wheat in the Midwest. Tractors of this era were brutes, designed to haul heavy loads or pull large pieces of equipment. The emphasis was on draw bar horsepower and not on maneuverability. They were 100% gear and clutch driven, and in many models, the gears were not synchronized. This was not efficient for doing precision landscape grading of confined properties. The accessory implements were also limited to front-end loaders and scraper blades that were either rear or front mounted. A further complication was that most tractors had hydraulic and power takeoff systems that worked only when the clutch was engaged. These limitations had major impacts on the productivity and quality of work that could be done on a landscape project.

Frustrated with these restrictions, Sperber instructed his mechanics (actually kids who liked to work on hot rods) to reengineer one of his tractors so that it would be hydraulically driven, would go as fast in reverse as in forward, and would use a lever to switch from forward to reverse (this eliminated the time-consuming task of clutching and switching gears). He also asked them to move the scraper blade from the front to the rear and had them redesign the blade so that it was curved and had enclosed sides, which today has evolved into the omnipresent scraper box. The curved blade with sides was a stroke of genius, because the curve and sides allowed dirt to accumulate while the blade leveled high points and the accumulated dirt filled in low spots. It was a gigantic step forward in productivity and revolutionized landscape grading and leveling. Today's scraper box design looks simple, but building the original unit was not easy. ValleyCrest had no professional engineer. There was only a non-English-speaking Mexican mechanic who was a wizard with cutting, forming, and welding metal. Burt relates that the final success was accomplished by the tried and true method of trial and error; a triumph of the Edisonian approach to innovation of "keep trying until you get it right."

The innovation of a hydraulic-driven tractors and the box scraper gave Burt and his fledgling company a major competitive advantage over other contractors in the rapidly growing region of Southern California. Creativity became a hallmark of ValleyCrest. They successfully applied creative thinking to develop the branch office concept and best-in-class, human resource practices. The company that was started by a 19-year-old teenager over 60 years ago with a $700 investment, now records $1 billion in annualized sales and is recognized as one of the premier green industry companies in the world. This amazing success story was made possible because Burt Sperber had the vision and courage to develop his own technical expertise where none had existed previously.

UNINTENDED CONSEQUENCES

Sometimes events that have unintended and unforeseen consequences can take place in the name of progress. The impacts can be negative or positive depending upon one's location or situation. The banning of the pesticide DDT was good for the survival of birds of prey whose egg shells were affected by DDT, but DDT was a cost-effective method of controlling mosquitoes. Its elimination had an unintended, devastating impact on hundreds of families whose children died from malaria carried by mosquitoes that would not have existed if DDT had not been banned. Another unexpected consequence of progress gone awry is well known if you live in the South. Kudzu, native to Japan, is an aggressive climbing vine that was brought by the U.S. government to the southeastern portion of the United States to reduce soil erosion and provide forage for farm animals. The growth and spread of the plant, however, was explosive. Now found as far north as Pennsylvania, it is classified as a major weed and is considered an ecological threat that smothers and crowds out all native plants. What seemed like a good idea at the time, Kudzu has grown into a tangled nightmare for farmers, municipalities, and utility companies. Under favorable growing conditions, the vine can grow over 12 inches daily. The best laid plans and intentions can sometimes have unintended frightening consequences. Before launching new projects, professionals need to thoroughly research their plans for progress and discuss their proposals with others.

In the case of the banning of DDT, the unintended result was a resurgence of malaria-bearing mosquitoes. In the business world, positive intentions can have unforeseen impacts that occur without warning. Some can be positive and others downright scary. Just like the mute head of a Jack-in-the-Box that pops out at you with its frozen smile and stares back at you when you turn the corner of the aisle at your local store, you can find a competitor's product priced below your production costs. How is it possible to be in a price war with a competitor who is located 2,000 miles from your nursery and of whom you have never heard? This is not another case of manufacturers moving offshore to take advantage of low-cost labor and lax government regulations with unfair subsidies, but rather it occurred in the 1960s, and the competitor was located in the United States on the West Coast. Thanks to the Cold War, tax money made possible this reversal of fortune that happened to Barnes Roses, located in Heron, Ohio.

After the Korean War, the Eisenhower administration went on a massive superhighway building program to move troops and missiles throughout the country with an interstate system that bypassed towns and stoplights. The objective was to make the country more defensible by the rapid deployment of military convoys across state lines and to decrease traffic congestion in major cities. An unintended consequence of the new highway system was that it created competitive advantages for low-cost producers located in more favorable growing regions of the country. Because they were able to ship their products inexpensively by truck across country, the new superhighway system created winners and losers based upon where businesses were located geographically.

Roses to Begonia's

Paradigm shifts of the magnitude created by the superhighway usually take a long period to occur. In the Barnes's case, the handwriting was immediately on the wall and easy to read. With local retail outlets offering high quality, bare-rooted roses at prices less than Barnes's production costs, there was no choice other than to stop growing roses and to head in another direction. When one door closed, however, another door opened. They transitioned their nursery and horticulture business into one that focused on growing trees, shrubs, and ornamentals. The name was changed to Barnes Nursery, and through hard work and clearly defined goals, they successfully reinvented themselves.

The skill set that the Barneses developed during this transition was put to good use in later years when the challenge of recycling large volumes of biomass became an issue. This challenge was turned into another business opportunity. The development of a unique technical expertise was a key to the development of Barnes's next major enterprise, but it was not a linear transition.

Some people are born into a business, some start their own, and some are hired, but Sharon Barnes did it the old-fashioned way–she married into the business. At the time her sights were not on a career in the green industry, and especially not in becoming one of the foremost national leaders in composting. Her passion was to pursue her special-education degree in teaching. This she did for several years, raised two children, and then decided that she wanted to join her husband in the family nursery business. Because Sharon had no business, let alone any nursery experience, her first days on the job were case studies in humility and comic relief. Her first customer asked where the begonia section was located. Not only did Sharon not know where the begonias were in the store, she was not too sure what a begonia looked like. Sharon dutifully found another coworker to help her, and with this first step, she began her odyssey of becoming one of the premier technical experts in recycling and composting.

Compost Happened

As the nursery business grew, Sharon also matured into an accomplished nursery manager. Through the 1990s, sales doubled in just five years. This was great for business, but as a result of the rapid growth of their landscaping business, yard waste began to accumulate. This created major issues with the local authorities as Barnes Nursery was rapidly running out of storage space. At this point, Sharon became interested in composting as a possible solution to turn the huge mounds of yard waste into a value-added finished product. She began to research the subject and approached the horticulture department at The Ohio State University for advice. The Barneses were desperate to find an outlet for all their accumulated biomass and were intrigued with the idea of developing a new business venture that would convert waste into a salable product. Sharon was given the go-ahead to develop a master plan to achieve this objective. Because Barnes was on the leading edge of the green movement, there was not a lot of practical industrial information to be had beyond university research on the best practices for the production of high-quality compost. Sharon soon found that the best sources of information were other composters, but they were located throughout the United States. Sharon became actively involved with the US Composting Council and was selected their first president. In the process, she became a leading authority, traveling the country and visiting Japan several times, working to establish best-practice standards. From a befuddled salesgirl to one of the top composting experts in the country, Sharon Barnes made a huge transition.

The Ultimate Paradigm Shift

Paradigm is defined as a generally accepted model of how ideas relate to one another. When Sharon Barnes was choosing her major in college and a career, her realistic choices were limited to being a nurse, a secretary, or teacher. She chose to be a teacher, but ultimately ended up being a highly accomplished businesswoman. In the 1950s and '60s, and even more so in previous decades, women were not expected to go into business; rather, they were discouraged. During this same period of time, in a parallel universe, of which Sharon was not a part, the women's movement was gaining momentum. Although Sharon was not following the same path as the women's rights protesters on nightly TV, she arrived at the same destination. It took humility, courage, and determination to establish a new business and become a leader in the compost industry. The odds were against her - she had no formal business training, no technical education, and she was a woman in a man's world. A pioneer, in every sense of the word, Sharon's accomplishments were achieved because she taught herself to become a technical expert and ventured forth to become a true professional.

THE INNOVATION EQUATION

The entrepreneurial professional organically tends to be on the driving side (left) of the innovation equation rather than the reaction (driven) side:

Opportunity (synthesizer, left to right) → New Product
New Product ← Challenge (reactor, right to left)

Sometimes, however, because of technical innovations or geopolitical developments that have occurred beyond their control, entrepreneurs find themselves on the wrong side of the equation. Examples are the diesel engine replacing steam power, hand-held calculators making slide rules obsolete, and Hispanics changing the workforce. This is what happened to Barnes Roses when the newly created highway system allowed the shipment of low-cost roses. The Barnes family could have become victims with their heads buried in the sand and gone out of business like the Baldwin Locomotive Works and carbon-paper producers when copiers and word processors were invented. Instead, they leveraged their nursery background by positive reactions to the challenge and drove the innovation equation to the left by creating an ornamental-plant business based upon the technical expertise they had developed growing roses. This experience served them well when they went to the left-hand side of the innovation equation and capitalized on the opportunity of converting waste biomass into a marketable, high value, finished product. Professionals who have sound technical expertise can work both sides of the innovation equation and control their own destiny either by identifying and capitalizing on opportunities or responding and adapting to challenges.

Innovation Versus Creativity

Innovation and creativity are many times used as interchangeable synonyms. These descriptors have two distinctively different definitions, in my opinion. Creativity refers to the ability to generate new ideas, visualize new art forms, and to develop novel concepts. Innovation is the reduction of ideas to practice. My definition of innovation in the business world is the reduction of ideas to profit.

A 40-year research study on creativity conducted by Dr. E. Paul Torrance has yielded some fascinating results. The project was known as "The Torrance Test of Creative Thinking" and is considered one of the premier studies on the subject of creativity. Two important findings have been discovered in the course of this research - the first is there is not a direct relationship between creativity and intelligence, and the second is there is a strong correlation between children who show creative talent early and adult success as entrepreneurs, inventors and heads of innovative organizations.

There is debate in psychological circles regarding whether creativity and intelligence are part of the same thought process. Researchers suggest the correlation between intelligence and creativity is not necessarily linear. While the results are mixed, it is generally accepted, in this discipline of study, that there has to be a certain level of intelligence for creativity to occur (but not necessarily related to high levels of intelligence). In other words, the higher a person's IQ does not mean that an individual will be correspondingly more creative. The good news is you do not have to be a genius to be creative. Creativity can be enhanced through education and training, and practice. Many people who feel that they are not creative can be provided tools and taught techniques that improve their imaginative skills, and it is not unheard of for these individuals to become quite creative when they find their area of passion.

It's interesting to consider the relationship of early childhood creativity with later success in the area of innovation. This seems to parallel the thesis of Malcolm Gladwell in his book, ***Outliers: The Story***

of Success, in that 10,000 hours are needed to master one's craft. Both this book and Torrance's research study strongly suggest that having creative skills in childhood would seem to give an advantage to those who pursue careers requiring imagination and originality. This does not prevent the creative 'late bloomers' from being successful entrepreneurs, inventors, etc. – they just have to work harder to catch up.

LOVE AND CREATIVITY

A dilemma that I have observed, which is counter to popular wisdom, is that being creative and generating a lot of new ideas does not ensure success. The creative part, even though it may be difficult, many times can be the easiest step of the process. The hard part is reducing an idea to practice. The challenge is there are so many variables in the innovation process - the makeup of the team, motivation and skill levels are just a few of the unknowns. A fatal flaw I have witnessed is many individuals and project teams fall into the trap of mindlessly generating ideas. They become obsessed in a constant loop of idea brainstorming - a cyclone of activity but never progressing from Ground Zero. They fall in love with the generation of ideas versus doing the work of innovation. This is what I call the wild boar paradox - they love the excitement of conceiving new ideas or concepts, but, once the thrill is gone, they are nowhere to be found. The work of gestation, birthing, and nurturing the project is left to others while they are off to other pastures to start the process all over again. I believe this syndrome is responsible for more project failures than most entrepreneurs realize. Sometimes you can have just too many ideas! It takes discipline and focus to manage the idea generation process so that it does not become an end unto itself. I hate to admit that early in my career I was guilty of this behavior and believed that throwing out a lot of ideas, the more the better, was helpful when in reality it was just the opposite.

Mentors

The importance or good fortune of having a mentor cannot be over emphasized. In my case, my early mentors (some may say role models) were my two grandfathers. One was a farm boy who transformed himself into a best-in-class, small-business entrepreneur and innovator, and the other, also a farm boy, transformed himself from Texas Ranger to world-champion livestock breeder and showman. Both had college educations, a rare feat for country youths at the turn of the 20th Century, and the first ever in their families to earn higher education degrees. The other two individuals who helped shape my education and career were my college advisor, Dr Wilber A. Gould, and my first boss, Ralph A. Miller, at Campbell Soup Company. They were instrumental in forming my views on what it takes to be a professional. They were models of professionalism and self-made individuals who came from humble beginnings. It was a privilege to receive their gift of themselves.

Mentorship is actually a modern version of apprenticeship. Mentors can come in many forms, whether they are relatives, educators, work colleagues, friends, or hired professional advisors. They all serve important short/long-term functions and make indelible lifetime marks. This is universally understood and accepted and has been common at universities through alumni, within fraternities and sororities, and within trade organizations through members. Big Brothers Big Sisters of America is an excellent example of mentoring in the volunteer sector.

Equally important to having a mentor is being a mentor, which can be rewarding for both mentor and the mentee. Having a meaningful impact on someone's life is a priceless gift that is fun to give. When you are being a mentor, the old adage, "It is better to give than receive" is true. Opportunities abound - churches, youth groups, schools, and volunteer organizations are always looking for help. Step up to the plate and give of yourself. You will be rewarded in ways that you would never have imagined until you mentor someone. It may even save your life. Alcoholics Anonymous reports that people who reach out and sponsor other members, stay sober longer and refrain from falling back into old behavior patterns. Alcoholics Anonymous is a peer group whose members understand the power of mentorship.

An intriguing aspect of being a mentor is that it does not have to be a one-way street where there is a master and student. Sometimes the relationship can be master to master, student to student, or an enduring partnership of equals built on respect and admiration for each other. Many times, students can be inspirations to their more senior mentors. My pre-teenage granddaughter, Hannah, is a born-and-bred, New-York-City girl, but she inherited her great-grandfather's love of animals, especially horses. When young, I worked with practically every other four-legged, farm-critter that existed but never with horses because when I was Hannah's age my grandfather traded in his show team of Belgians for a red-bellied Ford tractor. When Hannah visits the family farm, she teaches me how to take care of horses and shares her passion for them with me. She is quite an inspiration to watch, mucking out the horse stalls and struggling with 5-gallon buckets of water. Hannah, you are my mentor.

PARTNERSHIP OF EQUALS - MENTORSHIP AT ITS BEST

When Jerry Grossi was in college at Michigan State University, he would team up with Ed Dudgeon, a fraternity brother who had a side business of promoting rock concerts. This business venture eventually failed, but Jerry found a business partner for life. Ed was an Ohio farm boy who was butting heads with his father over farming the same piece of dirt, so Ed joined Jerry at Spartan Maintenance, a condominium complex management company. They eventually bought out the owner and expanded into irrigation installation and lawncare. Their business was incorporated on April 1, 1976, and has been a long-term partnership built on trust, equal sharing of work and a genuine like for each other. This has been a joint mentorship for a lifetime.

Peer Groups - Formalized Mentoring

A peer group made up of like-minded business people from across the country is a form of mentoring that helps to facilitate the process of benchmarking and networking. Jeffrey Scott's book ***The Leader's Edge*** is a good guide on how to form a peer group and maximize the benefits of sharing management and business practices among professionals.

Problem Resolution

As discussed in Chapter II, solving problems is hard work, but it can also be maddening when trying to resolve complex personal, professional or business related problems that involve other people with varying levels of technical expertise. Sometimes it seems that even the elements are against you. It is like being caught in the middle of a terrible storm with low lying clouds, rain and wind blowing in your face, and its being so dark that you lose your sense of direction and equilibrium. Sometimes, however, just when you think there is no way out and have no clue how to solve the problem, a bolt of lightning strikes, illuminates the surroundings and, in an instant, you can see clearly your position and a solution. Many times you have to weather the storm before an answer is forthcoming. Most issues have solutions, but sometimes it takes lightning strikes to help you find them.

Sharon Barnes admits to having a rather unique process for learning and solving problems. She is a people watcher, and she pays special attention to those she admires the most. She watches and studies their reactions to successes and tragedies. She tries to model her behavior based on the best qualities she has observed in others. This is what she did in elementary school, and, using knowledge from her special-education major in college, she improved upon her learning style and continues to use it.

THE THORN AND A KING

> One day a king was out walking when he stepped on a thorn, which hurt a lot and made him mad. He was so angry that he ordered one of his assistants, who was responsible for the roads, to cover all the pathways in leather so that this would never happen again. The assistant gravely suggested to the king that it would be simpler and less costly if the king covered his feet with leather. Sometimes one's first reaction to a problem is not the best solution, even though it may have come from a king. Seek advice from those who work with the problem on a day-to-day basis and listen to what they say. The assistant had courage when he suggested an approach that was different from the king's; the king could have ignored the suggestion and ordered, "Off with his head!"

This story makes for an interesting conundrum to the approach used for problem solving. The king's approach was to solve the problem at the macro level and to throw money at it. He did not give much thought to the issue at hand, which was his sore foot, hurt from a thorn. He did not want to have that painful experience again. Lacking any technical expertise on the subject, but being in control, he ordered the first thing that came to his mind. This type of thinking occurs when there is arrogant ignorance, and sometimes happens with high–ranking executives and government officials who are out of touch with the actual work that has to be done. A shotgun, one-size-fits-all approach may appear to solve the problem, but actually creates a bigger problem making the cure worse than the disease. This happens when the federal government makes and enforces blanket rules to be imposed across the country with little regard to local conditions. The same thing is true for corporate officers when they implement dictatorial, universal mandates on regional branches without considering unique regional differences and client needs.

Landon Reeve's approach to problem solving is to break down the process one step at a time and to get input from individuals who are living and working with the problem. He suggests that a common mistake in problem solving is skipping from the problem directly to the solution without addressing the overall cause of the problem. Landon explains, "If you fail to identify the root cause of a problem, your solution will likely be a temporary one, so it's important to think the process through and identify all the issues each step of the way."

CHAPTER V

Social Skills

***No one needs a smile as much as a person who fails to give one.
—Unknown***

We've all heard the adage, "You only have one chance to make a first impression." Google has 75,000 results for that exact phrase (and another 50,000 if you change "have" to "get"). What is really striking when one reads through those results is this: while it may seem personal and social in nature, it is a business concept. Making a good first impression is about getting the job, making the sale, or staying in the consideration set of any competitive process.

How does one make a good first impression? Along with the way you speak (Chapter IV - Technical Expertise), your appearance (being well groomed, having a good posture, and dressing appropriately) conveys a tremendous amount of information. These visual cues will either work for or against you, in ways neither you nor the person with whom you are interacting may be aware. As you are reading this, you may be excusing your lack of attention to these first-impression makers because of your confidence in your abilities and successful business/career skills. If so you are, however, missing the point. Your success does not mean that you could not be more successful. With regard to first impressions, truth is irrelevant: perception is the co-pilot for reality. While it may seem artificial or insincere, perception is the low-hanging fruit in the equation, so grab it. I do not suggest that there is a direct relationship between an individual's appearance and level of competence - a clean-shaven, nicely outfitted person can be technically inept and lazy. An unkempt appearance, however, immediately brings into question one's credentials and likely presents an unnecessary barrier to winning the job.

Mr. and Mrs. Manners

There is no excuse for any professional to lack good manners. Schools now offer courses in basic business social awareness - Business Etiquette 101. Several years ago colleges were receiving complaints from business recruiters that students were showing up for interviews inappropriately dressed and groomed. Even worse, when they were invited to off-site interviews (such as dinners), they did not have a clue why there was more than one fork alongside their plates. Even high-octane MBA graduates were showing up for work with the social awareness skills of sixth-graders.

Having a professional appearance and a semblance of social skills is vital in any business environment. It starts with the job interview, whether you are being hired or the one hiring. If you are not dressed appropriately, you are raising questions that do not need to get raised. Who wants to buy from salespeople who are poorly groomed and look like they slept in their clothes? If you have the appearance of a rejected loser from a TV reality show, your loan application at the bank is not going to make it off the loan officer's desk - let alone be approved by the loan committee. Would you go to work for an individual who looked more like a homeless person than a prospective employer? The answer is probably not, unless that individual was Howard Hughes. If you are going to attract top-level professionals, you must look like one.

Personal Brand

Anyone in sales or marketing knows the importance of branding. The logo, the name, and the color combinations are all critical in conveying a first impression and identifying a company or its products. So critical are these factors to product identity that the U.S. patent office issues trademarks to protect brand names and logos. The Rolls-Royce name is more valuable than that of Hyundai. This is also true for people's individual identities. I do not think it will be anytime soon that the U.S. patent office will issue trademark registrations for peoples' appearances, but nonetheless appearance is important in conveying one's persona and image to the world. Your identity is unique: it is like a fingerprint - no two are alike, so guard it carefully - it must last you a lifetime.

I learned this lesson in a college classroom. It was not in a textbook, nor was it part of an assignment. It came in the form of me being used as an example by my college professor. In an introductory course on food technology with over 30 students in the classroom, the professor (while lecturing on the importance of branding food products) pointed at me and said, "Hildebolt there - I always recognize Bill because of his long hair (actually my hair was no longer than John F. Kennedy's who was President at the time). I can always pick him out in class." When he later became my advisor, he told me that he had not meant his comment as a compliment. I found the whole thing somewhat curious because my advisor was bald, wore bowties, and white socks. The point is that appearance (just like a product's packaging) is part of an individual's brand. Teddy Roosevelt had his top hat and General MacArthur his corncob pipe. How is your appearance contributing to your personal brand?

Social Skills - The Stealth Advantage

All else equal, being equipped with good social skills will give you a distinct advantage for building a successful career and advancing to the top ranks of an organization. This is especially true for people such as politicians, executives in large corporations, and education administrators. In today's instant media world, appearance and sound bites have premium values. Even exceptions to the rule are instructive. Donald Trump is a self-aggrandizing, brash, real-estate developer and reality TV star. He is not a role model for manners - unless his persona is as fake as his hair. He is not, however, successful in a large corporation or other collaborative role. He would not last five minutes inside P&G, Google, or any other business that depends on teamwork. Even his fame is a direct result of his behavior being impossible to emulate because it would be a fast track to the unemployment line for the rest of us. Unless you have a rich daddy or have inherited vast sums of money, social skills are critical to your future success. This is not confined to high executive levels. Entrepreneurs and other small business owners, including those of us in the green industry, need sharp social skills in order to be successful and build positive relationships with customers, employees, vendors, and bankers. Small businessmen do not have business cards with Fortune 500 brands on them to help pre-deliver a first impression, so if your manners are crude and your language vulgar, you will be forced to look elsewhere to make a living. Pro wrestling comes to mind.

BE WARY OF FIRST IMPRESSIONS

Even as you understand peoples' tendencies to be swayed by first impressions, be careful not to judge people based on first impressions. I learned this lesson early in a freshman chemistry class. Across the lab bench from me was a student who was so thin he actually folded up on himself when he sat down. I thought to myself, "This kid isn't going to make it - no way. He won't even be able to cross campus without being blown away." Even more telling, he did not look that intelligent, if intelligence has a look. Wow, was I wrong. I may have been like some people whose first impressions of the Wright brothers was that they could not build bicycles let alone build and fly an airplane. It was not too long before my skinny lab mate was working at his own bench in a professor's lab. Later, I found out that he was one of the top students in the chemistry department and received an invitation to conduct independent research. In short, he was a genius.

Making judgments based on first impressions leaves you vulnerable. If you underestimate a potential competitor (like my chemistry classmate) you may put yourself in a situation in which you may be the loser. If you are fooled by a falsely positive first impression, you may find yourself dependent on a weak employee or vendor. Because none of this is conscious, it takes time for you to realize your mistake as many people have learned the hard way.

First impressions can produce four kinds of results: 1) a positive impression that is reinforced as you get to know the person, 2) a positive impression that has a negative result as a relationship develops, 3) a negative impression that is confirmed with further interaction, and 4) a negative impression that turns positive over the course of time. In scientific terms, first impressions can result in a true positive, false-positive, true negative, or false-negative. With an initial personal judgment, a person has as many ways of being wrong as being correct. The probability of success is dependent on many factors - the first and probably most important one being how perceptive a person is at deciphering voice and body language clues. For this, females appear to have better perception skills than males. They may not have a monopoly on reading people, but they seem to have better intuitive senses when it comes to interpersonal relationships. Another variable is the subject's personality, and how successful the subject is at projecting the desired image. Even though I am conscious that first impressions can miss the mark, I still misjudge people. My example of my fellow chemistry student was a false negative. In a relatively short time, I learned that he was a "positive."

Left Brain, Right Brain

We had an opening for a marketing/bookkeeper position in our office. I have since painfully concluded that accounting and marketing require two entirely different skill sets that are rarely possessed by one person. Accounting is a left-brain function whereas marketing and being creative are right-brain functions. If you ask right-brain dominated individuals to keep your books and do your accounting, and left-brain dominated individuals to write your ad copy, you will end up with unpaid bills and droll ad copy. Assign one person to perform both functions and it is likely neither task will get done well. This would be a bit like teaching pigs to sing. The exercise would annoy the hell out of the pigs, and when they finally learned how to carry a tune, it would be an awful noise. Over the course of hiring about five individuals, we finally learned our lesson. The job functions were separated and given to two different people who possessed the correct brain orientations. Now, our marketing programs look professional, and we do not have vendor calls inquiring about late payments. I am embarrassed to admit that it took me about 10 years to figure this out.

Returning to first impressions, as part of the hiring process, our office manager would screen several candidates until she found someone she really liked and would schedule that person for an interview with me. One such interview involved a young lady who was employed by a local bank in its IT group. The lady was doing computer work, although looking back she was vague on the details. The bank was a large, well-known institution with well-trained and respected employees. When questioned about why she wanted to change jobs, she indicated a dislike for working in a large bureaucratic organization. She said there was a lot of politics and no opportunity for advancement. She also mentioned a willingness to take a substantial pay cut to be able to work in a position where her skills would be better employed and appreciated. She also liked the idea of working in a family-owned business.

After another round of qualifying interviews, our management team weighed her positive and negative attributes. On the positive side, she possessed computer expertise, writing experience, a professional demeanor, a good personality and experience working with clients. On the other hand, we could not verify her references (they were either too old or just personal friends), and for obvious reasons, we could not call her present employer.

Still, one question lurked unanswered in the background: why would someone intentionally agree to a pay cut of several thousand dollars? When put on the scales of blind Justice, the attributes and experience tilted in her favor, but the real clincher was that our office manager "loved" her. I scheduled Susie (name changed to protect the guilty) for a final interview and decided that if she accepted the salary and terms of the job I would hire her. Susie readily agreed to our terms. I told her that she needed to give her two week's notice to the bank and that she could start to work on the following Monday. As I described for Susie more of the job details, I commented, "Most people we hire grow into their jobs, but in your case, I think that you can actually grow the job." Well as Paul Harvey used to say, "Now, for the rest of the story." Two hours after Susie left our office, we received a call from her boss at the bank. "I understand that you offered Susie a job," she said to my office manager. "Susie has given her two week's notice, but since we are overstaffed anyway, she can start for you immediately."

When the office manager stepped into my office to tell me the happy news, all I could think was "This does not bode well." My instincts were correct. The next day Susie showed up on time - a good sign, but she parked her car at a funny angle in the back of the parking lot. Being naïve me, I asked a dumb question, "Susie, why are you parking so far away?"

"Oh," she replied, "My transmission will not go into reverse, so I've had to park like this the last several months." Her car's mechanical defect was a mirror image of her life; she had no reverse, no neutral, and no common sense - just full speed ahead! Her computer skills turned out to be mediocre, and her first attempt at a newsletter looked like a psychedelic, cut-and-paste scrapbook from hell. I tried to politely explain that her version of the newsletter, while innovative, creative, and a real eye catcher, was not what our conservative clientele expected to see from us.

I also pointed out that it was a major departure from the format that we had been successfully employing for the last 10 years. Her response was that I was "mean."

Susie neither grew the job nor grew into it. The chaos and extra work she created far outweighed her contributions. Her nonperformance and erratic behavior were like a runaway train, and the inevitable wreck occurred on the night of our 10th anniversary dinner/dance party. Here, she proceeded to get drunk and brag about (and then show off) her $3,000 enhancement surgery - to the delight of our male employees and the mortal disgust of their girlfriends. Having left the party at a reasonable time, I did not get an eyeful, but I definitely got an earful the following Monday.

I fired Susie, but the story does not end here. One of the offended parties called first thing Monday morning to heap some abuse on our Saturday night, amateur-hour stripper. When told that she was no longer with us, the girlfriend quickly asked if the position were open and, if so, could she apply for it. It was, she did, and we hired her. Unfortunately, the cycle started all over again. This time around, the offense was less about over exposure and more about over use - of a company credit card.

I hope that I have made a compelling case that first impressions are a topic worthy of thoughtful consideration, from both sides of the table. On the sell side, making a bad first impression is like stumbling out of the starting blocks in a race: it is difficult to recover, and on the buy side, allowing a first impression to cloud mask the real situation can lead to a variety of expensive mistakes.

ATTITUDE

"Your attitude will determine your altitude in life." Zig Ziglar

Attitude - everyone has one; it is just that some have good ones and some have bad ones. I personally think that a person's psyche, including his or her prevailing attitude, is largely determined at birth and that one's environment (either negative or positive) can influence one's attitude over the short run - it is, however, difficult to change one's genetic hard-wiring over the long term. This means that maintaining a good, healthy attitude is more of a challenge for some people than it is for others. One of the more inspiring stories about how a positive attitude can affect one's life comes from Viktor Frankel, a Holocaust survivor. Frankel survived the horrendous life of a Nazi concentration camp on sheer determination, his positive attitude, and spiritual well being. By thinking of his wife, he was able to fight to stay alive and not lose hope. From his experience, he observed in the concentration camp that it was those who had nothing to live for who died first. Dr. Frankel later became a psychiatrist and a well-published author on the subject of positive thinking and how the human mind can overcome huge challenges. If a positive attitude can help a person survive a concentration camp experience (during which all of the person's friends and relatives are killed and the person has little hope for survival), imagine what a positive attitude can do for a person who leads a normal life. On the flipside of this motivational story are a number of people who have incredible skills/talents/athletic abilities, but fail to live up to their potential. Their negative attitudes poison everything, including their own potentials. Everyone knows someone who fits this description: I know I do - I am related to a couple! The truth is if you do not have a positive attitude no one wants to be around you in either a social or business setting. Unless you were born into royalty and riches (and the odds of that are remote), you need to work on developing a positive attitude.

The Cleveland Twins

There must be something magic about Lake Erie water that creates positive attitudes and can-do spirits. Both Jim Paluch and Phil Fogarty were born and raised in Northern Ohio close to Lake Erie. The two are close friends and have such similar characteristics that one thinks that they were twins separated at birth. Both found distinguished careers in the green industry: Jim, as the founder and head of JP Horizons (a highly respected consulting group specializing in teambuilding, motivation, and lean management principles) and Phil, as the owner and operator of a Weed Man lawncare franchise. They are high-energy, dynamic leaders and are creative innovators in their respective fields.

JP Horizons, along with Ariens, were the first companies to bring training programs on lean management to the green industry. They have had a major impact on a multitude of companies by helping them to work smarter and improve their overall operating efficiencies. Fogarty has been active in industry association work as a volunteer and was the originator of PLANET's Renewal and Remembrance Day of Service at Arlington National Cemetery where over 200 acres are spread with limestone each year. This event has grown into a major volunteer effort, and, in 2009, NBC Evening News featured Phil Fogarty in its "Making a Difference" segment that was broadcast nationwide. Jim and Phil have the can-do spirit and positive attitude that enables them to truly make a difference in the industry and the people with whom they work.

PERSONALITY

Many years ago, when I was in the corporate world, my boss sent me to an executive grooming school located in the Colorado Rockies. Prior to attending this weeklong course, I took a personality test. While I do not recall many of the details about the results, I vividly remember the instructor's reaction when she reviewed them. She exclaimed, "You have the same personality profile as my ex-husband!" Out the window went any personal coaching for the week. It seems that her ex and I shared a somewhat rare and seemingly annoying characteristic (to her at least) of being an introvert with strong, creative tendencies, and even stronger ability to visualize. As she explained, we were both "off the charts" on the vision thing and she seemed to take delight in explaining this "defect" in detail. "You visualize things so strongly in your mind that you think there is no need to explain a thought or concept," she told me. "Even worse, people like you sometimes visualize ideas to the extent that you are convinced you've already shared your ideas with others when you haven't." When I later told this to my wife, she further annoyed me by agreeing with my instructor. This was an important insight about my personality - an aspect of it that I continue to struggle to overcome.

From this intense week of self-assessment exercises, I learned quite a bit about the differences between introverts like Bill Gates and extroverts like Bill Clinton - to simplify, the former gains energy from actually working on a concept in a solitary environment whereas an extrovert feeds on the energy of a group. Both types have important places on your staff and team. During meetings, the extroverts drive the discussions, throw out all kinds of ideas, and talk constantly, while all the time gaining more energy as they interact with others. Their counterparts, the introverts, observe, think, and process the information. At the end of the meeting, the introverts are the ones most likely to best synthesize the essence of the discussions and bring the meeting to a productive close. The challenge, of course, is to get the introverts to actually contribute. Once you do, they will usually offer a well-rounded perspective about the subject at hand. The key is to make sure that everyone, both the extroverts and introverts, are given the opportunity to express their thoughts. This means sometimes questions need to be directed to those who are not speaking up.

In life as in physics, for every action there is an opposite reaction. If positive energy flows in one direction then a negative flow occurs in the opposite direction. When extroverts are forced to do introspective work, they have to expend a great deal of energy focusing and concentrating to remain on task. In other words, they have to work harder than if they were in a social exchange. The same theory applies to introverts who can be friendly (once they get to know you) and, with effort, become great public speakers, politicians, and leaders. They just have to focus a little harder than their extrovert counterparts. I witnessed this counterintuitive phenomenon at the Colorado leadership development course. As I listened to the numerous lectures throughout the week, I marveled at how outgoing, friendly, and spontaneous the two lecturers were who headed up the program. The lady who said I had the same personality profile as her ex-husband was one of the instructors, and I was especially observant of her.

As the weekly lectures, team exercises, and evening sessions wore on, an interesting thing happened. Initially, both the male and female lecturers were bubbling over with enthusiasm and high-voltage energy; they created excitement and electricity in the air. I had them both pegged for off-the-chart extroverts. By midweek, though, subtle changes appeared. The determination and focus were still there, but the bounce in their step was gone along with their perpetual smiles. By Thursday, they were approaching ground zero, still very professional, still presenting great material, but the magic (the spark) seemed to be extinguished. By Friday, the wheels had come off. Their hair was a mess and even their clothing looked rumpled. They had hit the sound barrier and were tumbling sideways.

Later that day, during their concluding remarks, they both confessed, almost apologetically, that they were actually introverts. Although they loved lecturing and teaching, a weeklong course drained them of all their energy. They went on to say it would take them a week or more to recover. I had been fooled yet again, but I smiled to myself as I managed to figure out why the lady instructor's marriage likely failed. I said to myself, "Like forces repel or perhaps their relationship lacked balance." I may have been off base with my assessment, but it made me feel better. Being married to an extrovert for more than 40 years, I can say with some experience that balance is good for a marriage.

PERSONALITY TESTING

Personality is probably the most studied, talked about, and analyzed psychological factor in the business world. There is an entire industry built around testing, analyzing, and placing people based on their personality scores. This science (and that is what it has become) has come a long way since the mother and daughter team of Catherine Briggs and Isabella Myers developed the Myers-Briggs Type Indicator personality inventory test in 1942. This method places people on a sliding scale for the following traits: extroversion or introversion, sensing or intuition, thinking or feeling, and judging or perceiving. A person's personality is determined by how the person scores on these various indicators. To predict preferred working styles and how people will perform in teams, numerous refinements to this test have been made by other consulting services, but the fundamentals of the test remain the same as they were when the test was developed over 60 years ago.

For the last several years, Swingle Lawn, Tree & Landscape Care has been employing personality tests to help understand the makeup of its leadership team, and the company president, John Gibson, continues to think that this, when used properly, is an excellent tool. "It can be especially helpful in areas where understanding an individual's personality traits can be beneficial in resolving conflicts, improving communication, and overall balancing a team." He warned, however, against the temptation to pigeonhole individuals because of their personality test results. Someone who is tested as a strong introvert may actually end up as a top salesperson because the person possesses great technical knowledge and the natural ability that gains client trust and builds relationships.

The Babushka Doll Syndrome

John also cautions against selecting team players in your own image. He explains that one has to fight this tendency inorder to ensure team balance, "If everyone has the same educational background, took the same subjects in school, attended the same schools, read the same books, and had the same grades, they would be a direct reflection of each other and ultimately of yourself. "When this dynamic occurs, and it often does, someone or everyone is ultimately redundant."

An apt metaphor for hiring employees in your own image is the Babushka, a traditional Russian toy that has a series of decreasingly-sized dolls placed inside one another. Each is a smaller clone of the other. If every individual fits into the mold of the boss, the organization is going to be an ever -shrinking team of increasingly less competent members. This is how redundancy becomes systemic and a part of the culture. If everyone thinks and acts alike, the net result is a lack of diversity, perspective, and the ability to create dynamic change. Similar ideas within similar thinking create stagnation and leads to obsolescence.

Returning to the example of John and his football playing days, if he only recruited blocking full backs in the image of himself, he would not have an effective team. It may be a team that Machiavelli would have loved, but with players whose main responsibilities are to knock other people down, it would be difficult to succeed in the 21st Century. Every organization needs players to block and run interference, but the organization also needs players who are able to run through holes, throw, and catch balls on offense and use a different skill set on defense. Diversification is the key. The rules of the game change depending on which side of the ball you are on, and you can never be certain which side you are going to be required to play.

TEAM OF RIVALS

Doris Kearns Goodwin in her Pulitzer Prize winning book *Team of Rivals* describes how during one of the most turbulent times in American history Abraham Lincoln selected his strongest political rivals for his Cabinet. People thought this first-time President from Illinois was crazy and naïve to bring into his inner circle of trusted advisors the very people who had run and campaigned against him in the Republican presidential nomination process. This bold decision turned out to be a stroke of political genius and was ultimately the determining factor in Lincoln's success in guiding the nation through a perilous period. The diversity of Lincoln's cabinet ensured that multiple views and ideas were presented and discussed before a final decision was made. If Lincoln had selected his Cabinet in his own image, the nation today would most likely be very different - frightening to contemplate if what happened in Eastern and Central Europe are indicators of what could have been. I am certain there would be no Lincoln Memorial overlooking the National Mall. Diversity is important in both businesses and governments. The professional entrepreneur understands this and works hard not to replicate him or herself in their enterprises.

Interpersonal Skills

Unless you happen to be an exceptionally skilled brain surgeon or a computer programming genius, having good interpersonal skills will be a prerequisite to success. Being able to communicate effectively is critical when running almost any business, building teams, dealing with customers, and, yes, even when negotiating with your significant other. If you lack interpersonal skills or the will to develop them, you might as well stop reading, because without them, you are not going to be successful as an entrepreneur or professional. Too many competitors have these talents and too many customers have come to expect good interpersonal skills for you to survive without them.

The first axiom of interpersonal skills is to appreciate people for who they are and what they do. People do not want to be taken for granted; they want to be recognized and respected as individuals. This is true for employees, customers, friends, and family. This is easy to do, and it begins by simply applying a golden rule that is as old as recorded time.

- In ancient Greece this guiding principle was "do not do to others what would anger you if done to you by others" Isocrates 436 -- 338 BC

- "Never impose on others what you would not choose for yourself" Confucius 551 -- 479 BC
- Islam: "Hurt no one so that no one may hurt you" Mohammed 570 AD

After more than 1,500 years of evolution, this philosophy was captured in the Catholic catechism, "do unto others as you would have them do unto you." With so many different cultures and religious sects teaching this principle over time, it is difficult to comprehend why so many people have not learned to practice this simple truth. By now one would think it should be part of every human being's DNA. Unfortunately, this is not the case anymore than it was in ancient times. The important point to remember is that if you ever find yourself in a situation in which you do not know how to act, apply the Golden Rule - it is universally accepted and priceless!

THE ART OF LISTENING

An interpersonal skill that is becoming a lost art is the ability to listen and actually hear what others are saying. Most people focus on formulating a reply to what is being said, rather than listening and understanding what is being said. A successful communicator develops a talent for listening carefully, processing the information, and replying with an intelligent answer. This binaural ability is what separates the professionals from journeymen in sales, human relations, or any other situation in which understanding other persons' positions are critical. Half listening produces half-baked responses. It is a simple process - listen to what people are saying and respond accordingly, but this is easier said than done, as evidenced at almost any business meeting. A good way to show you listened is to rephrase what you heard and ask, "Is this what you are saying?"

Here is another lesson I learned the difficult way. When I was at Campbell Soup, I hired the first female research technologist and later the first female development manager, who were the only female professionals in product development; so when I joined RJR, I had limited experience working with female employees. However, there were many females throughout the R & D department at RJR, and one of the first promotions I made was to appoint the first female research-and-development vice president to my staff. This was one of the best moves I ever made, and it definitely broke any latent Babushka doll tendencies that I may have had. Then reality struck.

Being the head of a large research organization had many challenges, but there was one particular challenge I had no clue how to handle. My superior had an open door policy that I tried to emulate and that meant there was a constant stream of one-on-one meetings with employees. Most meetings were requests for manpower support or funding and occasionally trying to resolve interpersonal staff issues. Many of the visitors were females and when the discussion turned to problem solving, being male and thinking that I was being helpful, I would offer suggestions and recommendations. Wrong! I later learned somewhat embarrassingly from my newly promoted VP that this is not what my female colleagues wanted. Actually they did not want to hear from me, they just wanted me to listen. Another lesson learned the hard way.

Life Balances

In previous chapters, I talked about the technical aspects of being a professional. In review, being a professional requires having technical expertise, a good work ethic, strong personal character, and social skills to be able to communicate with associates, customers, and other individuals and groups with whom you do business. All of this is balanced by and dependent upon having a healthy attitude about life and being in good physical and mental health. To achieve this balance, one must take a holistic approach to one's life. With any occupation, there will be times when work and work issues monopolize the day, the week, and entire months. Weather, customers, employees concerns and making ends meet are all part of being an entrepreneur, and the sum of all of it can be very stressful. Making and keeping one's balance in life is a virtual juggling act

EGO - REALITY VERSUS PERCEPTION

After only one song on the TV show "Britain's Got Talent," the British overnight singing sensation, Susan Boyle, at age 47, dramatically demonstrated that there are wonderfully talented, undiscovered people all over the world. Because of circumstances, they never had the opportunity to exhibit their talents for which they could be recognized and appreciated. It is important to keep this in mind and to maintain a sense of humility no matter where you are in a social or company hierarchy. There are many Susan Boyles out there capable and ready to take your place.

Anyone with a camcorder, in the Internet age, can become a worldwide sensation. In previous generations people's identities existed only within their own local communities. Today, we live in a big world with billions of people, but it is a small world when it comes to information transfer, so the probability is high there is someone who has superior skill, intellect, and ambition to do what you think only you can do. The barriers to information transfer have fallen so dramatically that talented people can both find and pursue the opportunities that best leverage their skills and passions. Depending on your energy level, this can be either an opportunity or a threat, so stay humble and on your toes, or you may embarrass yourself. Another aspect of talent to remember is everyone you meet can do at least one thing better than you – even if it is just surviving in a cardboard box.

***"Oh Lord it's hard to be humble, when you're perfect in every way". -* Mac Davis**

Years ago a famous ad executive made a statement that the best way to communicate a message is to put it to music. All of us have been there and done the following at some point in our lives, so the following verses from songs are meant for those who sometimes fail to keep their lives in balance and in perspective.

In the song *Big Shot*, Billy Joel sings, *"So you wanted to be a big shot, you had to be a big shot didn't you, you had to have a white-hot spotlight."* Sometimes our egos and self-importance become bigger than reality. If you are humming in your head the lyrics *"No one does it better than you"* by Salt-n-Pepa, and it comes out *"No one does it better than me,"* your business colleagues are most likely singing to themselves Carly Simon's *"You're so vain, I bet you think this song is about you, don't you?"*, and your closest friends are thinking of Judy Collins's *"To send in the clowns; don't bother they are here"*. Once achieving the "white-hot" spotlight that is so desired, reality is summed up in a Neil Diamond song about a frog that dreamed of being king and became one, and in the end Peggy Lee asks, "*Is that all there is?"* In these verses, I am trying to sum up a message suggested by Shakespeare that life is a stage and we can choose to be humble servants or fools.

The opposite of being humble is being arrogant. A colleague recently pointed out that for an arrogant person to become humble, it is frequently necessary to experience humiliation as this is often the only way the proud and arrogant are brought to a place where they can eventually embrace humility and become teachable. Like Icarus flying too close to the sun on wings made of wax and falling into the sea, the "white-hot" spotlights of fame, riches, and position have melted a multitude of highflying egos over the intervening centuries. It's best to develop a sense of humility early in one's life and career so it becomes a core value. Humiliation is an equal opportunity teacher and no one is immune, so learn your lessons early and avoid embarrassing yourself later in life. Humiliation can also be an effective deterrent; the government uses the "perp" walk in front of flashing cameras and TV reporters when arresting white-collar criminals as a message to their colleagues in crime. Hopefully you'll never have to do a "perp" walk, but embarrassing yourself in front of family and fellow professionals is just as painful.

Keeping a balanced perspective is sometimes difficult, especially when friends, family, work colleagues, and if you are a sports star your fans keep telling you how great and successful you are. It is hard work to keep yourself grounded in reality because even though you happen to be successful in one aspect of your life, it does not guarantee success everywhere else.

Success is sometimes a result of being at the right place at the right time. Talent and hard work help, but sometimes achieving success is like winning the lottery in that success can depend upon who your parents are, when you were born, where you were raised, your race, and social class, etc. Hard work and perseverance increase opportunities for success, but even though the peasants of China and Mexico are hard workers, they are trapped in a subsistence existence. Be humble - it is easy to over inflate one's achievements and importance. Appreciate the God-given talents that you have, employ them wisely, but always keep in mind that God did not give you a monopoly on these talents. Finally, recognize that success is often fleeting and based more on perception than reality. Stay grounded. It is important to be true to yourself and to know your strengths as well as your weaknesses. Be sensitive to the views of others, and be aware of others' perceptions of you. To be comfortable in your own skin, you must feel good about yourself and have confidence in your abilities.

PASSAGES

When you are growing your company or working hard to run an ongoing business, keeping life in balance is a literal juggling act. Later in life, it is also important to know when it is time to stop being the juggler and to move off center stage. Here is how one industry veteran accomplished this.

When Landon Reeve first started Chapel Valley, his goals were relatively simple: to become a respected professional in his industry and to own and operate a high-quality landscape contracting business. It is obvious that after 41 years, he has fully achieved these goals. He is now turning the business over to his two children. At this stage of Landon's career, he considers himself more of a mentor than an operating manager. He wants to stay involved in the business but not run it. He is enjoying seeing his son and daughter grow into their respective positions and carry on the family business. Reeve believes in continuing education, as indicated by the numerous conferences and education venues he has attended and continues to attend. This veteran places a high priority on keeping healthy and fit and is focused on his personal wellness. He likes to travel and is taking advantage of this time in his career to take trips with his wife and family.

Human Being Versus Human Doer

An executive recruiter once asked me if I were a human being or a human doer. This caused me to have an epiphany that changed my view on how I was living my life. It made me realize that sometimes it is easier to just be robotically doing as opposed to dealing with the messy human elements in an organization.

Starting in the 1990s with user friendly PCs and accelerating through today's always-connected smart phones, the speed of life (both personal and professional) is approaching warp speed. No business sector has survived unless it has made the quantum leap into this ramped-up electronic superhighway. Everything has sped up: microwave food, Google instant information, 24-hour newscasts, round-the-clock shopping, and social media innovations that create constant contact opportunities. All of these changes have occurred in a relatively short period of time, and the only restriction on even more rapid increases is how fast electrons can be squeezed through wafers of silicon. We are not built to process information at this rate of speed and evolution will probably not keep pace with such rapid changes in our environment. No wonder it is hard to keep the "being" in human being!

STAGNANT SALES EQUAL STALE EMPLOYEES

Once the focus of doing gets ingrained in a company's culture, it is difficult to change. When your business is accelerating and growing at a rapid rate, it is a challenging process, but it is also an exciting time. People are focused on their work, and knowing that company growth equals salary and career opportunities, they are energized. When you are traveling at the speed of sound, your primary focus is on what is ahead of you instead of internal details. As my mother-in-law used to say, "No one is going to notice a spot on your shirt when you're riding a galloping horse." When the growth in a business stops, however, and a downturn occurs, the same phenomenon happens that occurs inside a rapidly climbing airplane as it noses over and goes into a downward dive - everyone in the plane experiences weightlessness and disorientation.

Jerry Grossi explains that during the last economic downturn, this is what happened to Arbor Lawn, his company located in East Lansing, Michigan. After a decade of solid growth, he had to deal with more than the external stagnation of the local, auto-manufacturing-driven economy; he had to focus more attention on the morale and mental focus of his employees. Because of the lack of growth and decreased revenue, promotions and raises became difficult to fund. Good employees, through no fault of their own, were essentially running in place, and this was true for both short-term and long-term employees. With opportunity restricted because of a depressed market, the challenge was to figure out how to keep employees motivated and mentally and physically on the job. It took creativity and strong leadership based on trust and openness to meet this challenge. It also took a well-refined understanding of human nature.

Equilibrium Point

Dr. Phil Allen is a natural force both in his professional and personal lives, which are blurs of kinetic energy. As a professor at Brigham Young University, he built one of the best landscape horticulture departments in the country. When I asked him what he sees unfolding next in his life, he became reflective and referred to Thoreau's teaching about the importance of simple living in natural surroundings. He went on to say, "One of the things I am thinking about lately is that there are negative costs associated with pure busyness, and we can easily be caught up in things that matter little. When I immerse myself in nature and spirituality, it helps me to recognize what matters most." This is coming from a person who has set high goals throughout his life and worked hard to achieve them: he ran 70 miles/week to become a competitive, long-distance runner; completed a four-year college degree in two and a half years while working multiple jobs; and during 20 years, changed a nondescript horticulture department into one of the best in the world. Watching Allen in action makes the Energizer Bunny seem like a sleeping koala bear. As a top educator, Phil practices what he teaches and has been able to find the equilibrium point on the teeter-totter of life.

Don't Be a Boiled Frog.

Keeping a life balance and perspective is important, but sometimes we cannot become too comfortable or fixed in our views of the world. If you place a frog in boiling water, it will immediately, out of reflex, jump from the container. If the same frog is placed in cold water and gently heated, the frog will sit passively, adjusting to the increased temperature until it is cooked. Professionals and successful entrepreneurs must be sensitive to their environments and respond accordingly to changes in the economy, technology, competition, and labor issues. Ongoing adjustments are always necessary. Do not wait for the near-death experience that the U.S. auto industry went through in the 1970s, while the Japanese auto manufacturers gained market share and the hearts of U.S. customers. Detroit did the equivalent of rearranging the deck chairs on the Titanic as it sunk. They focused on marketing and sales gimmicks and ignored that the fact their products were poorly built, overpriced, and inferior in design and reliability. This happened over the course of many years, and it was not until they realized (as alcoholics sometimes realize) they had reached the bottom and changed their ways. How telling it is that even with thirty years to recover, GM and Chrysler were both forced to go through bankruptcy in 2009 to survive and address fundamental flaws in their businesses.

According to Landon Reeve, the key is to success is to survive and to achieve this, one must respond responsibly to changing business dynamics. Either you intelligently make necessary adjustments, or you reduce your ability to operate.

THE PROPRENEURS GUIDE TO MAINTAINING BALANCE ...

Responsive

Responsive actions must be responsible actions. The English proverb 'look before you leap' is as true in business as it is in personal life. The difficulty is in making the right decision at the right time. When you think a downturn is about to occur, reacting too quickly to cut back labor and marketing expenses can create lost opportunities and allow your competition to surge in front of you if the downturn does not occur. Procrastinating and hoping that the market is going to turn around can have equally devastating consequences if a slowdown does occur. Remember the boiled frog. Depleting cash before the economy does improve is self-inflicted suicide. It is important to keep your antennas up and your early warning systems active. This can be achieved by attending technical conferences and talking to trusted mentors and friendly competitors, particularly those in other parts of the country. Do not be provincial and focus on your local market only; trends in other parts of the country can be early indicators of what the economy and business opportunities may be in your region.

Flexible

Being responsive also means that you have to be flexible. By definition entrepreneurs are flexible; they adapt to changing times and make good with less than perfect situations. If key employees are sick, entrepreneurs do not panic; they re-arrange their schedules and pitch in where necessary. They may have planned to be in their offices, but if workers or tractor drivers are needed, entrepreneurs change their schedules to accommodate the situations. They create order out of chaos and thrive on the challenges of solving problems at multiple levels. If equipment breaks, they do not fume and curse - instead they make repairs and correct the situations that created the equipment breakdowns. Clients cancel for reasons - entrepreneurs consider such cancellations as learning experiences and try to prevent the cancellations from happening again.

Flexible also means that you have to be open to changes in technology, social morals and mores, and employee and client expectations. Years ago, it was rare to find women in the green industry workforce. Now it is not uncommon to see female crew leaders and lawncare technicians. It is difficult to change old habits, especially if you work in accounting and record keeping. Twenty years ago computers and spreadsheet software changed the playing field, and in some cases the game. No longer were a number two pencil, a big gum eraser, and your CPA degree sufficient to keep you competitive with your peers. The power of instantaneous recalculations and formatted worksheets switched the command position from those who had the mechanical abilities to accurately, neatly, and manually record data to those who could work a keypad and think abstractly. The same phenomenon took place with the advance of computer-aided-design software, which allowed smaller companies to compete with much larger companies that had staffs of landscape architects. Because everyone could pretty much afford the same software, the playing field was leveled (sort of like a nuclear arms standoff), and the competitive advantage switched to those companies that had the most imaginative and creative employees. The adage that you cannot teach old dogs new tricks is not as true today as it once was. Senior citizens and senior managers (the baby boomer generation) have embraced the computer and e-mail as did their grandparents and parents the telephone and TV.

Agile

A characteristic parallel to flexibility is agility. Being flexible means that you are willing to adapt--being agile means that you can execute being flexible with precision. It is more than just being quick on your feet - it is knowing where the rocks are when you are trying to walk on water (that is, you need to be prepared and do your homework in advance). The trick is to be able to take a full-body slam, jump back to your feet, and quickly recover your equilibrium. To be agile, you have to be lean both in person and in business. It is difficult to maintain one's balance when you are carrying extra weight, and if there is waste built into your system, it is going to be a hard journey with excess baggage. It becomes a daunting task if you are carrying a 900-pound monkey on your back. Your footwork is going to be slow and prodding.

Resilient

The pros who make the all-star teams and the superstars who survive their journeys are those who are the most resilient. Staying in the game is a top priority. Winning or losing is not as important as how you played the game and staying in the game. If you get knocked down, do you get up, and get back in the game? If you fumble the ball, do you sit on the sideline with your head buried in your hands, or do you go back into the game and finish what you started? Taking hits and getting up to fight on is the key. This is what makes a professional a pro.

Humor

Building a new company and/or career is a long journey with a lot of delays, detours, fender benders, and all-out crashes. There are constant obstacles along the way, so having a sense of humor and positive perspective makes the journey much more pleasant. Loving what you do and having fun even though you may encounter setback after setback provides the strength to persevere. To laugh and smile in the face of adversity maintains self-confidence and a positive attitude. In big games, the star players are laughing, smiling, and cracking jokes to channel their energies and calm their nerves. Professionals love challenges and relish opportunities to compete against the best in their professions, and they do it with humor and smiles on their faces. President Lincoln told funny stories and jokes to his discouraged cabinet members and generals to help ease the tension during the gloomiest days of the Civil War. He did this not only to convey positive messages, but also to help maintain his own mental well-being and focus.

Grace

A sense of humor is made more genuine when the person is warm and sincere with his or her colleagues. This creates an atmosphere of joyfulness that permeates day-to-day activities. The crowning jewel that exceptional professionals possess is the rare commodity of graciousness. A gracious person has the sensitivity and skill to be considerate of other peoples' feelings and carefully chooses the words they speak and the actions they take. They are polite and kind without appearing weak or condescending. Gracious individuals are humble in victory and generous in defeat. Any individual who masters this characteristic is amazing.

The First Wealth Is Health - Emerson

The same characteristics that define a professional also apply to ones wellness.

Expertise - understanding basic nutrition and the role of exercise is critical in determining one's long-term health. Your genetics play a big role, but the important thing to remember is that you have no control over who your grandparents and parents are, but you do have complete control over the food you eat and the exercise you do. There are many conflicting diet theories that have been made popular by a whole range of weight loss programs and pills that are aggressively hustled by scam artists who use surface mail, e-mail, and TV. There is an abundance of good research and scientific data available regarding diet and nutrition, but unfortunately, there is an equal or greater amount of junk science. Unless you have a medical condition (such as, diabetes, high blood pressure, or allergies to certain foods), you do not have to be a nutritionist or visit a nutritionist to eat healthy. All you need to do is consume a balanced diet of protein, fat, and carbohydrates. Avoid high-fat foods and those with high levels of refined sugar or salt. Not all fats are bad; fats such as omega-3 fatty acids (which are present in abundance in some seafoods) are essential for good health. Fats are also essential for the digestion of fat-soluble vitamins - such as vitamins A and E. Carbohydrates are important sources of energy and essential in the digestion of proteins. A balance of vegetables, meat, seafood, grain, and dairy products consumed in moderate quantities makes for a healthy diet. It is important to have breakfast, and eat balanced portions of proteins, fats, and carbohydrates at each meal.

The concept is simple: if you have a healthy weight for your body frame and you balance the calories that you eat with the calories that you use, you will maintain your weight. It is also critical to your total-wellness program for you to exercise to keep your muscles and cardio-vascular system well toned.

Although diet and exercise are critical for maintaining good health, genes also have a role. It is important that you get regular physicals and that these become annual once you are in your 50s. These can be supplemented with checkups, as needed. When I was in my early 30s at Campbell Soup, I had advanced to a level where annual physicals were mandated by the company's medical director. Dr. Weir was an early pioneer who recognized that high cholesterol was a sign of potential heart disease. He was known around the company as a cholesterol Nazi. If your blood tests indicated elevated triglycerides and cholesterol, he immediately placed you on a diet and recommended exercise. If that did not work, he prescribed a disgusting tasting, cholesterol-reducing medicine. People who ate in the executive dining room sat far from Dr. Weir to avoid lectures and reprimands on their eating and lifestyle habits. All of my ancestors are of Northern European stock, primarily German and Irish. As a consequence, I seem to have genes that are associated with risks for high cholesterol and high blood pressure. When I had my first annual physical, Dr. Weir told me my cholesterol levels were so high that I needed to start taking a cholesterol reducing medicine immediately. I did this and also began to more closely monitor my diet. This greatly reduced my cholesterol levels, and because of this, I have been on a continuous diet and medicine regime for the last 30 years. I look back on this and thank Dr. Weir, without whose intervention, I may not be alive today. I can say this with a certain degree of certainty in that my two-year younger brother, Dick, was not fortunate enough to work in an organization that required medical physicals. Just over two years ago he died of a massive heart attack. Later in life, he did have annual physicals but by that time the damage had been done.

Too Much of a Good Thing

One of the unrealized dreams that Phil Allen set for himself as a teenager was to make the U.S. Olympic team as a distance runner. Dr. Allen was, and still is, a high-energy individual who has a Western-frontier determination. While in high school, he often ran 10 miles a day, and as part of his training regimen, a neighbor convinced Phil that if he ate only vegetables, he could run faster; so Phil became a strict vegetarian and continued his 70-mile-per-week training program until in the middle of a cross country meet he began hallucinating that he was being chased by demons - he ended up in a fetal position in a snowstorm. Not only did this experience teach Phil the importance of conditioning his body for long distance running through proper nutrition, but this incident also scared him because it made him think that he might have inherited the mental illness that was present in his family. This had a profound influence on his view of the future and how he should prepare himself for life. He knew that he would have to maintain balance both in nutrition and exercise.

Hard Work - The discipline to maintain a proper diet and exercise program is hard work. With all the distractions of business and family issues, it is easy to grab a fast-food meal rather than prepare a healthy meal, and it is much easier to watch something on television rather than go to the exercise gym where you made a six-month payment and to which you made a commitment to visit daily. In a TV advertisement for a cholesterol-reducing drug, a heart attack survivor who is reflecting on his lifestyle that led to coronary disease asks, "What was I thinking?" In the past, other things were more important to him than his health, which he took for granted and assumed would always be good. His focus was on enjoying the present and short-term crises, not on his long-term well being. The question is: was this person uninformed about the relationship of health with diet and exercise or was he too busy or lazy to care? Whatever the answer, the end result was that his health suffered, which can lead to a permanent disability or even early death.

STRESS - THE ULTIMATE KILLER

Just surviving in today's modern world is hard work. When the added pressure of raising a family, making a living, starting a new job, or creating a new business is added to this mix, both physical and mental stresses are magnified. Some stress is beneficial as it helps keep us energized and focused, but too much stress creates major problems. Stress can drain your energy, cause you to lose focus, and be bad for your health.

Constant stress can cause serious psychological and physiological damage and can be a killer. Headaches, weight gains, cardiovascular diseases, and even cancers are associated with the toxic byproducts produced by stress. To assure your well being, you should use a holistic approach that includes diet, exercise, relationships, anger management, and how you deal with disappointment. Anger creates stress and stress releases free radicals that can cause cell destruction and in some cases cell mutations, which are the precursors to cancer and other medical problems. Disappointment can lead to self-induced anxiety, which is a forerunner to stress. Being unorganized and failing to properly plan can cause stress. Procrastination in dealing with an issue in a timely manner can produce tension, which can quickly escalate into a stress overload. The ability to handle stress is one of the distinguishing features of a professional, but equally important is organizing one's life so stressful issues are under control and can be managed in a positive manner. Success is largely perception, and in many cases, so is stress. There are real stresses in life and business without creating your own due to poor self-management. It is often challenging to separate life's real stresses from those that are self-made. Pay attention to the cause of stress in your life and work to remedy the reasons instead of reacting to the stress.

Personal Character - Some people can be described as having addictive personalities. Whether or not there is a genetic component to such personalities has yet to be resolved, but we all know people who rely on nicotine, caffeine and alcohol as coping aids. Almost anything in moderation (the poison is in the dose) is not going to harm you, let alone kill you, but if you become addicted to certain behavior patterns, there are well-known negative consequences. To break these habits takes strong willpower, a close network of friends, and in some cases, medical intervention. The best policy is to avoid overindulgence in the "sinful pleasures" of smoking, drinking, overeating, and binging on foods such as desserts and chocolates. To start these behaviors at a young age can set up destructive patterns later in life. The best rule is moderation. In defense of the sinful pleasures, if they are consumed in moderation, they can actually result in healthy pleasures that have positive benefits on one's physical, psychological, and emotional well being. Although the causes of the benefits are still being investigated, a number of studies have found that drinking red wine (the French paradox) is beneficial, and resveritrol (found in the skin of red grapes) is now being sold in health-food stores. The beneficial anti-oxidant properties of chocolate are also being investigated.

THE SHOT TOWER EFFECT

Many factors influence one's character, but ultimately it is the passage of time that has the greatest impact. This is a natural process in one's journey from youth to maturity. It is also a gradual process that requires endurance and an accumulation of experiences to achieve a healthy life balance.

Prior to the 1780s, lead shot (used in muzzle loading rifles) was made with molds. This process was labor-intensive and inexact. If the lead shots were not perfect spheres, rifles would not function properly, and once fired, the shots had unpredictable trajectories. The solution to making round shot a routine process was as ingenious as it was simple: molten lead was passed through a hole in a copper plate which formed droplets that after falling 150 to 260 feet into a pool of cool water were perfect spheres. The surface tension of the molten lead formed precise balls as the droplets fell, and the spheres were solidified when they hit the water. The longer the fall, the more perfect the spheres. The building that was used for this process was known as a shot tower and was invented by a British citizen named William Watts.

Over the years the surface tensions of daily life in both personal and business affairs have the same effects on peoples' characters and social skills - the rough edges are smoothed and polished. Not all people are turned into perfectly formed persons, but most of us have our rough edges somewhat smoothed. All it takes is time and positive attitudes. This analogy is not exact, as a person cannot freefall 150 feet into a pool of cold water and come out well rounded. For the propreneurs this is a process, an accumulation of experiences, education and interpersonal relationships, and when this process reaches full development, it is a thing of beauty, the rough edges are smoothed, false vanities and egos are buffed clean, and what remains are the core values of one's character. The end product may be good or bad, but the process almost always produces a more mature and wiser person.

Social Skills

One's appearance and attitude are directly correlated with one's health. Healthy people have robust appearances and positive attitudes. They feel good about themselves and this confidence is reflected in their interpersonal relationships and communications. Having healthy bodies creates healthy minds. It starts with taking care of yourself and understanding that what you consume whether it is food, drink, or drugs becomes you. You are what you eat and drink.

Sustainability

The sustainability of environments and the sustainability of profitable business models are hot topics, but I consider them to be of secondary importance compared with the sustainability of health. If people are not healthy, they will probably not be able to build long-term sustainable environments and businesses, and even more important, they will not be able to provide long-term support for their families. People can have all four legs of their professional stools in balance, but this is for naught if they do not have balanced lifestyles to ensure that the fruits of their labors are lasting.

EPILOGUE I

"And God said, let the earth bring forth grass, and the herb yielding seed, and the fruit tree yielding fruit after its kind, whose seed is in itself, upon the earth and it was so" – Genesis 1:11

Regardless of religious preference, most of us would agree that life exists because of a thin layer of soil, abundant sunshine, and rain. Because of the miracle of photosynthesis, we have food and shelter. We are quickly finding out, however, that soil, sunshine, and rain have to be in balance to provide life, and in today's modern world, this balance is tenuous. As members of the green industry, we are charged to ensure this balance and to protect our environment. We are in a privileged position to make a difference. Life on earth is a miracle, and it's a miracle we must work at together to sustain and even improve.

INTRODUCTION

to Profiles of Professionals

The Professional Entrepreneur

In the course of conducting the 12 interviews for this book, I uncovered a well-kept secret I only vaguely knew existed. What I discovered is that there is an elite guild so secret that members of this society do not realize their own inclusion, but they do recognize and admire fellow members. Entrance into this entre-nous* guild has neither gender, race, class, age, or occupation restriction, nor is there an application form or nomination committee to determine who is included. Membership is a selective and self-directed process and is achieved after years of hard work plus professional and entrepreneurial successes. Members in this guild are professional entrepreneurs. I use the term "propreneur" in referring to these people.

After careful consideration and much deliberation, I selected the following 12 successful business people and educators to interview. All are part of the green industry and exemplify the unique talents, characters, and accomplishments that are necessary to succeed in today's world. At their cores, these people are entrepreneurs who bring creativity, enthusiasm, and energy to everything that they do. They have mastered their crafts and professions. They are also, in my opinion, environmental heroes who are on the frontlines and improve the qualities of lives in the com-

---

**confidential, among us*

munities where they live and serve. They provide the services, products, and educations for their workers to make their communities better places in which to live. All have strong senses of stewardship for their families, customers, enterprises, students, the environment, and people in general. This is what makes them propreneurs.

I could have selected to interview many other propreneurs with equally compelling success stories, but my intent was to keep my book short and to the point, not to interview every propreneur whom I know. It is easy to recognize propreneurs when you meet them - they project self-confident, non-assuming auras. When two professional entrepreneurs meet for the first time, there is an instantaneous emotional and intellectual connection. When you fill a room with propreneurs, there is magic - much like a gathering of explorers and mountain climbers - neither bragging nor boasting but rather unselfish sharing of great adventures.

The following pages take you inside the lives and careers of 12 people who share the great adventure of becoming propreneurs.

CHAPTER VI

....

Profiles of Professionals

PHIL ALLEN

Business people measure their successes in terms of profits and losses, accumulated asset values and returns on investments. In the case of an educator, such as Phil Allen, the metrics of success are defined by his or her students - their educations, future vocations, and overall accomplishments in achieving balanced lives. This is a passion and avocation that has to be a core value, because there are no stock options, performance-based bonuses, and no commissions for producing highly educated, trained, and motivated graduates. The success and failure of any industry, and ultimately that of the nation, depends on the future generations of professionals and leaders, but there is no financial incentive given for the quantity and quality of students produced - just the reward and love of making a difference in the future of the nation's youth, one student at a time. A natural born educator and volunteer, Dr. Allen epitomizes the quote "mankind was my business" (Jacob Marley, ***A Christmas Carol*** by Charles Dickens).

Phil, the oldest of six children, was born into a family of educators and artisans. He grew up in Arizona, Utah and Wyoming, where he developed a passion for the outdoors as big as the Grand Canyon. His earliest memories were summers spent camping in the Utah deserts, where his dad worked summers as an extra and handyman on movie sets. Here Phil got to meet actors such as John Wayne and Ronald Reagan. The senior Allen's career, as an English teacher, was cut short when a bout of mental illness (bipolar disorder) impacted his ability to teach. The father moved the family to a small town in Wyoming and started a lumberjack business, harvesting lodge poles and pine logs in the summers and firewood in the winters. The business was a family venture that employed Phil, his two brothers, close friends, and cousins. It was hard and dangerous work, plus, as Allen explains, his father's talent was not business, so the enterprise made just enough money to keep food on the table. Phil did, however, learn important lessons: he would have to work hard to survive; he had a passion to live and work outdoors; and he had a distinct fear of business.

When Phil was a kid, the family did not have much money for vacations, so his main form of diversion was hiking, and he was blessed with wide open spaces and the beautiful landscapes of the Southwest. He felt like his childhood heroes, Tom Sawyer and Huckleberry Finn, and spent any free time he had exploring trails and camping. His sense of adventure and living in the wild was put to the test many times. After a wildfire, for three summers Phil's family cut lumber and damaged trees from a resort area, lived in a tent, and bathed in mountain streams. To make ends meet when there was a lull in the lumberjack business; Phil's father would use his patented process for layering sands (which he had gathered from throughout the western U.S.) between glass panes to make paintings. His mother did oil paintings of western and religious scenes. When they were on the road, the family would peddle their art at rest stops, campgrounds, gas stations, or wherever people would listen. Phil did not enjoy selling, doing cold calls, nor did he enjoy talking to strangers. He thinks his disdain for selling and calling on strangers was in part because when his father was in the manic phase of his bipolar disorder, he was an excellent, high-energy salesman and this made Phil nervous because he knew the depressed phase was not far off. During his missionary service while still a teenager, Phil was essentially forced to talk with strangers almost all day long, seven days a week and eventually overcame his dislike for talking with people.

The family did stay in place long enough for Phil to attend high school where he became a competitive runner for both the track and cross-country teams. He was also elected captain of the chess club, and he now realizes that playing a lot of chess at a young age helped him to think strategically as an adult. Another constant in his early years was the Boy Scouts, where he often spent 20 hours or more a week engaged in scouting activities and achieved the rank of Eagle Scout. One summer, when his father had a steady job (other than lumberjacking), Phil worked on the grounds crew at the school, and during another summer, he mowed lawns for a high school teacher.

One of the goals (which became an unrealized dream) Phil set for himself as a teenager was to make the U.S. Olympic team as a distance runner. Phil was, and still is, a high-energy individual with a Western frontier determination. While in high school, he often ran 10 miles a day, and as part of his training regimen, a neighbor convinced Phil, that if he ate only vegetables, he could run faster. So Phil became a strict vegetarian and continued his 70-mile per week training program until in the middle of one cross country meet he began hallucinating that he was being chased by demons and he ended up in a fetal position in a snowstorm. This scared Phil. Not only did he learn the importance of proper nutrition to condition for long distance running, but he also feared that he might have inherited his father's mental illness. This had a profound influence on his view of the future and how he should prepare himself for life.

The church had a huge influence on Phil's life. After high school, where he had taken four years of Spanish, he was selected by his church leadership for a two-year missionary assignment along the California/Mexico border where he worked with Hispanic migratory workers. Prior to his assignment, he spent two months in intensive language training at Brigham Young University. The experience he gained through his missionary work helped him realize that he had a talent for working with people who needed help and this gave him a sense of accomplishment. Recognizing the satisfaction he felt when helping others put Phil on a career path in which he would always be involved with people and make a difference in their lives.

When it was time for college, Phil went to Brigham Young University and chose psychology as a major. Part of the reason he chose this major was his desire to try to better understand his father's mental illness and to develop a stronger self-awareness. He described his college years as a time when he worked his tail off. He worked multiple jobs, in the evenings as a custodian in retail outlets and during the days as a grounds crew worker on campus. He attended classes non-stop and was able to graduate in two years plus one semester. Just prior to his last semester, a random event occurred in which someone suggested that, because Phil loved being outdoors and worked on grounds crews throughout high school and college, he should investigate horticulture courses. In Phil's style, wanting to maximize his last semester before graduating, he took three horticulture courses. This was a life and career-defining decision. He fell in love with horticulture and has never looked back. Based on these three courses, he decided to get a masters degree in horticulture with a focus on the sciences of plant pathology, plant physiology, and soil science. This led Phil to accept a graduate assistantship in turf science at the University of Minnesota. Part of the reason that Phil was attracted to study turf science was that he was still intrigued by the idea of being closely involved with sports, such as athletic fields and golf courses. His dissertation studies were on the synchronization of grass seed germination, and this resulted in his development of a patented process; European seed producers are still employing some of the ideas from his thesis research. After graduate school, Phil returned to Brigham Young University and joined the horticultural department in a teaching and research position. Here Phil continued his research into the physiological changes that trigger germination. Although he is still active in the lab, most of his current experiments are conducted in the field in

Utah, Nevada and Arizona. Some of his work is focused on a fungus that attacks seeds, and he hopes to develop a pre-emergent, weed-seed control for crabgrass, dandelions and poa anna. The objective of this work, funded by the USDA, is to determine if after wildfires these weeds can be controlled in wild-land areas in order to restore natural habitats. During their dormant periods, these weeds provide fuel sources for forest fires, and, thus, their control would help reduce the propensity for wildfires in the underbrush.

When Phil joined the horticulture department at Brigham Young University almost 20 years ago, there were 20 students enrolled. Presently there are 184 students majoring in landscape management. This makes the program one of the largest specializing in landscape contracting in the U.S. Much of the program's success is due to Phil Allen's dedication to his students and to the green industry. Phil credits much of what he has achieved to his involvement with green industry associations. When he attended his first Student Career Days event sponsored by the former American Landscape Contractors Association of America, now PLANET, he found that there was a big world beyond academics, and in his words, "I found what I did not know I was looking for." He says that the first seven years of his career were focused on his research, developing course outlines, writing grants, publishing, and obtaining tenure. He advised three to four students each year and had a major impact on their course and career selections; however, after being exposed to a much broader picture of the industry and what could be achieved by partnering with the industry, he immediately realized the opportunity to have a much greater impact on all of the students within his department. Brigham Young University became accredited by PLANET in 2003 and developed into an enthusiastic participant in education and student-recruiting events.

Dr. Allen is enthusiastic passionate partaker in everything he does in life. As he was finishing his Ph.D. program, he would run for stress release, and here he began to work on his racing endurance. He always had a personal goal to be a competitive runner in the amateur ranks and found in running he could bring balance to his professional life, and in the process, have more energy to perform his professorial duties. Beyond teaching, academics, and career training, one of his missions in life is to help students understand the benefits of having a strong appreciation of the balance between nature, academic pursuits, and personal health. He puts this into action by teaching a Career Planning course; students are given extra credit for following through on exercise programs. He is disappointed when he sees some students playing video games and living virtual lives while missing out on the beauty and miracle of nature. He encourages his students to go for mountain hikes, float down streams, prune trees, or do anything that requires that they be outdoors so that they develop appropriate balances in their lives and develop the tools needed to handle future life challenges. He suggests as a good read ***Last Child in the Woods: Saving Our Children from Nature-Deficit Disorder*** by Richard Louv because it describes how the children of today are missing out on the wonders of nature. Dr. Allen definitely does not have a nature-deficit disorder. If Phil has his way, Walden Pond may have a rebirth in Utah.

When Phil was asked what he thinks will next happen in his life, he became reflective, referred to Thoreau's teaching about the importance of simple living in natural surroundings and said, "One of the things I am thinking about lately is that there are negative costs associated with pure busyness, and we can easily be caught up in things that matter little. When I immerse myself in nature and spirituality, it helps me to recognize what matters most." This is coming from a person who has set high goals throughout his life and worked hard to achieve them; running 70 miles a week to become a competitive, long-distance runner, completing a four-year college degree in two and a half years while working multiple jobs, and taking a nondescript horticulture department to a best-in-class position in 20 years. Seeing Phil in action makes the Energizer Bunny seem like a sleeping koala bear. Phil practices what he teaches, and that is how to best meet the challenge of finding the equilibrium point on the teeter-totter of life. This is a challenge that even Tom Sawyer would relish.

DAN ARIENS

The name Ariens is one of the most trusted and recognized equipment brands in the green industry. Starting 75 years ago as a manufacturer of large garden tillers, Ariens is still privately held, one of the few equipment manufacturers in the green industry not publicly owned. The Ariens Company has always been an innovator and developed one of the first ride-on mowers in the 1950s, and in the 1960s, they started building snow blowers. Over the years, strategic acquisitions in Gravely, Stens, Great Dane, EverRide, and JT Thomas have made Ariens a well-diversified and internationally based company. Ariens has recently become well recognized and admired for their adaptation and development of lean-management principles. This latter initiative has been shared unselfishly with the rest of the green industry.

Dan Ariens is the fourth generation to head the company. Presently serving as CEO, he started as a teenager and climbed every step of the ladder - from assembly floor to corner office. Dan is the second son of nine children, so it was not preordained that he would ascend to the top position in the company. Younger brother, Peter, is the president of Stens - the parts supply division of Ariens. Dan has an excellent working relationship with his brother. They meet weekly on business issues, and at least once a year, they privately discuss their business and personal goals to keep open communication at all levels. Sometimes these meetings can last as long as four hours. The other siblings chose not to join the company and are accomplished professionals in other fields.

There are reasons few privately held companies, especially those the size of Ariens, have been in business for four generations. It is a difficult and challenging process. As any entrepreneur or family business owner knows, it is hard enough to survive the first generation, let alone successfully pass the business down four generations. It is a journey fraught with many obstacles; if inheritance taxes do not dilute resources, a defect in the family gene pool or a bad marriage will. Given the business cycle of the last 75 years, it is a wonder any business, private or public, could remain true to their founder's vision. With globalization, flat-world economics, and unfair foreign incentives, America's manufacturing base has been, and will continue to be, under siege. This is what makes the Ariens story so special.

During the 1950s, '60s and '70s, Ariens grew rapidly. As they expanded from their large pro-garden tiller base to consumer products (such as riding lawnmowers and snow blowers), they gained market share and name recognition. During this period, the company operated primarily as a family business both in structure and operating style. Dan's father, along with his brothers, ran the business and the grandfather was also a constant presence. The decision process was family oriented with family members focused on doing the right thing. Dan remembers that early on a lot of decisions were emotionally based; however, as the company grew larger, they transitioned to a more professional business model with the development of business plans and financial accounting. This was a difficult transition for some of the family members because for the first time they were asked to become professional managers, do their homework, and make tough decisions. Dan allows that this is similar to the patterns he sees today in family-owned contractors who are working to transition their companies to larger, more professionally-run organizations.

WHEN "THE BOSS IS NOT THE BOSS"

The difficult transition of moving from a family oriented business model to that of a more business driven process occurred under Dan's father's watch. As with any inner family dynamics, each individual brings a different level of passion and a view of the future to the table. This is made even tougher when you are working with close relatives such as your brothers. Sometimes the most challenging issue to resolve is when the boss is not the boss. A family member may be in a managerial position, but if he is not managing and leading the process, it leaves a void that other family members have to fill, or worse, the heavy lifting falls to a non-family subordinate. This builds resentment at all levels and makes it difficult to create a winning situation. Ultimately the best solution is for the family member to leave. This creates another family ripple, which impacts spouses, children, and parents. Dan credits his father for making this a successful transition.

Dan's career path was determined early, and by the seventh or eighth grade, he knew he wanted to join the manufacturing operations of Ariens. He fondly remembers his grandfather's influence on his life; he took Dan on assembly-line tours during which Dan sensed his grandfather's passion for the business. Dan's first attempt at assembling machinery was building a go-kart. He salvaged a small engine from the repair shop and was attempting to build a frame, when the guys in the R&D department observed Dan at work. They took this up as a stealth project and built Dan a first-class go-kart, so at an early age, Dan learned to delegate without really trying - a true sign of a future leader. Dan worked summers on the assembly line while he was in high school, and he continued in this role during his college years.

Dan graduated from St. Paul's College in Minnesota, and he recalls that his four years there were a challenge. The first year was a shock as he had to learn how to study and focus. The work was hard, and he allows that his first year was one of the more difficult transitions he has ever had to make. When he graduated, he was ready to go to work and start his career, but it was not with Ariens. His father had different plans. The rule was that Dan had to work two years with another company before he could join the family business. Dan landed a job as a road salesman for a Minneapolis-based company that sold fasteners; he pushed nuts and bolts, knocked on doors, and make cold calls. Lessons from the road taught him the importance of time management. He quickly learned that if he did not do his homework, call ahead, and set up appointments, he would waste precious time. If he needed to make six to eight sales calls per day, and only made four to six because of poor planning and scheduling, his commission-based income would suffer. This lack of planning was not a formula for success. Another challenge he had to overcome, which occurs with all junior sales people, was the tendency to talk too much and not listen to the customer. After two years of being a road warrior, Dan retired his sales case, parked the company car, and went to work for his dad.

Dan's first job for Ariens was as a product manager in marketing of consumer lawn equipment. His responsibilities included developing marketing programs and methods for selling to dealers. Based on what he had learned from his field experience, he was also supposed to send ideas to R&D. After having been on the road for two years as a sales rep, Dan had to undergo a major transition from being a solo operator to being a manager with direct reports and people coming to him for suggestions and directions. Moving from selling nuts and bolts to marketing a complete line of equipment was an eye-opening experience for Dan. He adapted quickly and, because of his earlier stints on the assembly line, he had a good understanding of and relationship with his employees. He also had the good sense to find a mentor who helped him navigate each step of the ladder as he advanced through the various departments (finance, receivables, manufacturing, engineering and eventually the president's office).

Keys to Success

Dan had this to say about success.

> Humility is the key. Many people assume, because you grew up in the business, that you know everything there is to know about the operation. If you start believing this and walk around the office with a swagger and arrogance, you're bound to make mistakes because no one knows everything about a company as complex as Ariens. Everyone makes mistakes, but if you operate from a platform of ignorant arrogance you're going to compound them. To learn, you have to work through the process, experience the hard knocks, and develop your own

leadership style. It is a process to develop as a manager because you have to build a leadership profile which is all your own. You have to gain the respect of others and to accomplish this; you have to respect them, too. Once this is accomplished, people will be more than willing to follow your directions.

The Legacy Continues

Dan and his wife, Julie, have five children - three boys and two girls. One son is working as an intern on Ariens' lean manufacturing initiative. Before his children are given plush air-conditioned company offices, Dan thinks they need to prove themselves by working for the company on the manufacturing floor alongside the workers doing hot and dirty labor. He believes this is the best way for them to learn what work is all about. He wants his children to get up early in the morning, be on time, and do what the workers do so that they appreciate what the other workers experience day in and day out. Dan believes the best teacher for a future leader is an end-of-the-pipe perspective working on the assembly line.

"The Holes Don't Lineup"

The first steps of Ariens' lean journey began roughly 30 years ago when the term "world-class manufacturing" was being touted as the salvation for the United States manufacturing sector. Dan well remembers this time because he was working on an assembly line as a seasonal laborer. He distinctly recalls that he was responsible for inserting axels into equipment frames, and on occasion, the holes did not line up. He used a mallet to force fit the axels into the misaligned holes. This damaged the bearings and wasted time. Dan was bothered by this, but throughout the company and deeply instilled in the supervisors was the operating attitude and mantra of "Just do it - get it done". No one on the production floor was allowed to question the process or make suggestions. No one ever asked, "How can this job be done better?" It was old school, top-down management with management knowing what was best.

The Journey Begins

At age 26, when Dan assumed the role of manufacturing manager responsible for over 600 people; his only previous experience in manufacturing was as a summer temporary worker on the assembly line. He clearly recalled his experiences on the line and understood that to make improvements in productivity and efficiency that production processes and procedures were going to have to be changed. Dan became a student of books published by Productivity Press and written by an industrial engineer named Shigeo Shingo, who developed the single minute exchange of die (SMED) process for Toyota. This was in the 1990s, and the Japanese using post World War II, Total Quality Management and statistical process control methods that were taught by Dr. W. Edwards Deming were well advanced in the process of continuous improvement in manufacturing. The best practices were being developed and executed in Japan, with Toyota the recognized leader. This is what Dan, therefore, studied. By the 2000s, lean management started to become embraced by other American manufacturers. "Lean" is a production practice that considers the expenditure of resources for any goal other than the creation of value for the end customer to be wasteful, and thus a target for elimination. Convinced by his observations that this was the right direction, Dan launched a full-scale commitment at Ariens to the development and adoption of lean principles. Later, based on the success of this implementation, Ariens teamed up with JP Horizons to teach these principles to landscape and lawncare contractors through the Working Smarter Challenge series, which has been hugely successful in teaching these concepts to the green industry.

Dan described his journey as one with no final destination. His objective is to never stop learning how to get better, become more efficient, and reduce waste. Over the last eight years, Ariens has been able to record a 12% annual productivity gain. They were also able to turn a business unit that was losing money into a profit center. To move from the old-school mantra of "just do it" to "do it right the first time" required a transformational process, which engaged everyone at every level from the office to production. This was accomplished through Kaizan events (events that result in improved processes) that continue today. Dan states that at least five years of structured training are needed for everyone in the organization before the learning takes hold and the transformation becomes an organic process unto itself. He emphasized that this is critically important because he and other managers cannot be everywhere and know all. To continually improve their own work processes, employees must be trained and trusted.

Crystal Ball

Although Dan predicts a positive future for the green industry, he does see challenges in the areas of regulation. Demographically, with the aging of the baby boomers, demand for exterior services will be ever increasing, but as long as the economic downturn continues, some growth restrictions will continue in the areas of residential and commercial landscape construction. He observes that in the past 20 years, the industry has come a long way, and he thinks that this trend will continue with people who make good products and provide good services continuing to do well. He is optimistic and even bullish on the future.

Dan reports that Ariens is presently in good shape, and, in the past 11 years that he has been CEO, they have made a conscious effort to balance their business units. They have moved from manufacturing complete equipment units to parts production, and with the addition of Gravely, Great Dane, and EverRide, they now have the diversity to weather the ups and downs of normal business cycles. Dan said he likes where Ariens is presently situated, and during the biggest economic downturn of recent memory, they have had no layoffs or shift shutdowns.

Dan and Ariens are generous supporters of the various trade associations within the green industry. Dan is currently chairman of the board of the Outdoor Power Equipment Institute and Ariens employees participate and contribute in numerous PLANET events.

Central casting could not do a better job in placing Dan Ariens at the top position of an American-legacy equipment manufacturer. He has an upper Midwestern sense of optimism, which is backed up by common sense and hard work. He has the self-assured confidence of a person who knows his strengths and is comfortable with his weaknesses. There is no sense of arrogance in his persona. He is the classic definition of a gentleman, with an engaging personality and a ready smile. He is the consummate professional in the green industry.

BILL ARMAN

Bill Arman began his green-industry journey at the age of 13 when his friend John Cox asked him to fill in as a mower while he was on vacation. When John returned two weeks later, he found that he was out of a job, replaced by the hard-working, more-dedicated teenager. Arman worked nine summers in a row in this position, and during this internship, he learned to enjoy working outdoors and doing physical hands-on work. As Bill puts it, he developed a passion for horticulture, and this has been a guiding principle throughout his professional career.

After high school, Bill earned a two-year associate degree from Pasadena City College, but he soon realized that a liberal arts education would not prepare him for his career goals. He wanted to follow his passion rather than follow money by getting an office job. He had heard from acquaintances that Cal Poly San Luis Obispo had a great Ornamental Horticulture department, so he transferred sight unseen and graduated with a four-year degree in 1976. Bill thinks this is one of the best things he has ever done.

Bill's first career-track job was with Green Valley Landscapes, which eventually evolved into ValleyCrest. His new boss had an enormous influence upon Bill's career and is one of the most memorable persons Bill has ever met. They, however, had a rough beginning. Upon hearing that Bill was a horticulture graduate from Cal Poly, Mr. Tak Ishida, a five-foot-four inch, samurai-style disciplinarian, exclaimed in a loud voice, "Ha, ha, horticulturists don't know nothing!" With this drill sergeant-type introduction, Bill began his apprenticeship under the master, Mr. Ishida. His first assignment was in the role of chief turf turd disburser (CTTD): he was given a backpack blower and was told to follow the mowers and distribute clumps of grass clippings left behind. As early as the 1970s, to avoid labor and landfill costs, grass clippings were not being bagged, so the residue needed to be evenly spread to avoid clumps from smothering the growing grass and leaving unsightly brown patches of clippings. Bill claims he became excellent at this chore and now considers himself as one of the pioneers in sustainable practices - recycling grass clippings in place.

Bill's nine summers working for an outdoor landscape maintenance contractor had conditioned him for the tough physical labor of a mowing crew. Located in the San Francisco area, there was a predominance of Hispanic workers, a trend that would sweep the rest of the country in future years, so he realized immediately that if he were going to be accepted, he would have to work as hard as the Hispanic workers did, which was no small task. He further knew that to be respected, he would have to work his tail off every day. Tak, impressed by Bill's efforts, overcame his bias against horticulturists and sort of adopted Bill by taking him under his wing. Once Tak had accepted Bill, the Hispanics quickly came over to his side and respectively referred to him as their "great white hope".

Tak was a California-born strawberry farmer, so he had deep roots in agriculture, and an affinity with nature that only people who have worked with soil all their lives possess. Because Tak was so impressed that a college guy had such a strong work ethic, love for the outdoors, and passion for plants, he arranged to meet with Bill on coffee breaks to discuss work and life in general. Like the cultivation of a bonsai plant (a slow and gentle process of shaping and forming), Tak helped Bill shape his vision for the future and set him on the right lifetime path. This act of kindness was based on respect and a desire to share one's talents with another being.

Once Bill had earned the respect of his coworkers and supervisors, it was a natural progression to be promoted to a foreman and soon after supervisor. Bill relished the opportunity to be the leader of his crew. He redoubled his efforts and continued to work as hard as the laborers he was now supervising. He wanted to be a role model who everyone would emulate. This is one of many classic challenges people encounter when they move from having hands-on jobs to being managers of other people. The usual result is that newly-appointed supervisors are reluctant to delegate and trust subordinates to do jobs properly, so new crew chiefs often try to do their jobs and simultaneously their subordinates' jobs while doing neither job well. This happened to Bill, whose struggle continued until one of Arman's clients (a property manager at a large apartment complex), took Bill aside and explained to Bill that he could not mow, trim, and manage his crew all at the same time and do the jobs well. This was an important jolt of reality. Bill learned an important lesson that what he was doing was not only wrong, but also it was difficult for him to move from being a laborer to being a supervisor. He had felt more secure and thought it would be easier doing the work himself rather than delegating the work to other people and trusting them to do the work correctly. This experience also taught Bill the importance of being receptive to coaching and mentoring. Bill said, "Seeking and accepting good counsel is paramount to one's success. Without it, it is easy to get stuck in the same groove and meander in a circle." A spinning top has a lot of movement, but it goes nowhere. A huge amount of energy is spent on creating centrifugal forces to keep the top upright, but there is never any forward progress. Without proper guidance, a supervisor may never move other than spin in circles.

When Bill started to focus on the leadership side of his career rather than the doing part, he had a clearer view of what he wanted his future to be and realized that he had the skill sets needed to achieve his goals as a future leader. At the time, Bruce Wilson was Arman's top supervisor, and Bill had witnessed Bruce's advancement path. This was when Bill started pushing the bubble. ValleyCrest was well established in Northern California but was struggling in Southern California. That is where Bill ended up next with his eyes wide open.

Bill was transferred to the Los Angeles area and found himself leading multiple troops in what he describes as a start up mode. The operation needed a lot of work, and Bill immersed himself in the process. He worked hard to recruit great team members and worked even harder to retain them. "You need great people in place if you are to accomplish great things." This was and still is one of Bill's main mantras. The new adventure had an exponential learning curve for everyone involved, including Bill; he had no formal business training, so it was on-the-job learning at warp speed. By the early 1990s, Bill was promoted to the regional VP for Southern California and was posting sales of $25 million annually with 500 employees and five business units located in six different sites. During this rapid-growth cycle, he, for the first time, had to budget, hold quarterly review meetings, and conduct weekly touch-point conferences at different locations. In the process, he built a best-in-class landscape maintenance operation and established a quality-assurance program that assured ValleyCrest would retain the best-in-class distinction among the many competitors in the LA market.

Bill remained in this position for approximately 10 years before being promoted to VP of Human Resources for the entire company. With the help of the McKinsey consulting group, he began to systematically organize the personnel procedures for the company. This involved totally revamping the performance evaluation process, implementing a metric system to rank employees, and identifying high-potential employees for further training and advancement. Over Bill's two-year tenure, he put into motion numerous programs to recruit and train top talent to fill the large number of new positions that were being created yearly by ValleyCrest's rapid growth. The demand for new employees was huge, ranging from machinists to horticulturists, landscape designers, and architects. Teams of recruiters were sent to colleges and universities across the U.S. to hire top talent.

The time spent in Personnel was another great learning experience for Bill, and it filled in a missing link in his resume. He had the hard-working part down pat, Cal Poly taught him the science, Tak the basics, and the school of hard knocks the business principles. Developing human resource procedures completed his education. His edges were smoothed and polished - he was the prototype model for the best-in-class, green industry executive.

Knock on the Door

In 2005, a Southern California landscape contractor niched in large development projects approached Bill and asked him to become president of a newly created maintenance division. He was offered equity and a competitive compensation package. Yearning to run his own operation, he accepted and within three years grew sales from $4 million to $8 million and increased gross margins 30%. Here Bill employed the same principles he had developed at his previous employer: his first priority was to hire the best people possible and place them in the right positions. This formula worked extremely well resulting in 20+ new hires in the middle management ranks, and this in turn helped drive rapid sales growth and operating efficiencies. Things were sailing along nicely until the economic downturn that began in 2007 took its toll. Because of the poor market, the owner reclaimed the presidency, and Bill was forced into the next phase of his challenging career. Bill had a long-held dream that once he was finished with corporate life, he would start his own consulting/coaching business. He now, unexpectedly, was given the opportunity. Bill's last day as an employee was September 11, 2007.

The Gardener Becomes the Head Harvester

On the evening of September 11, 2007, from a long germinating seed of an idea planted previously in discussions with Ed Laflamme 10 years earlier, Bill's first client signed a contract, and the Harvest Group was born. The name of this new partnership was deep-rooted in both Bill and Ed's passion for plants and people - helping hands to "harvest your potential." The slogan says it all: the Harvest Group was a marriage of Ed's entrepreneurial skills and Bill's corporate background, a hybrid of 70 years of combined experience. Their objective was to help clients build sustainable results while building equity and a legacy within each of their clients' organizations. They both had been at the top of the mountain in their respective fields and from this vantage point they were confident that they could help clients avoid the common mistakes made in the perilous journeys of building successful businesses.

I Knew I Had Made it, When

"I saw things that I had implemented, such as the quality assurance program, being adopted by other leaders in the company." This was an "ah-ha" moment for Bill, as he looked on with pride and said to himself, "It works." Bill gets great satisfaction from helping others become successful. He likes being a catalyst to make things happen. His proudest accomplishments are creating processes such as recruiting and coaching new hires, creating management cultures that have the clarity of expectations, and developing training programs that identify and groom future leaders and having these new processes endure long after his departure with recorded, sustainable successes. At the macro level, Bill estimates that his programs have impacted over 10,000 people.

In his role as a green industry consultant, Bill has helped numerous companies increase their gross margins. With returns of $3-$5 in profits for each dollar invested in consulting, the paybacks for the companies have been impressive.

Lessons Learned

Bill readily admits that some of his biggest mistakes were the result of his being too trusting and optimistic with some of his employees, especially direct reports. He attributes this to being overly loyal - a good trait for friends, but a liability that can be disastrous in a business situation. He uses an analogy of the coach who allows a pitcher to stay in the game too long. In Bill's case he waited too long to make the difficult decisions of replacing subordinates before they drove their business units into the ground.

Establishing the proper balance between being too nice and too tough is a difficult process. In business, as in life, people respond differently to different management styles. People are motivated differently, but there are certain basic truths. To varying degrees, everyone has spirit and heart; if, however, the management style is to squash everyone's enthusiasm and grind on everyone's spirit, the end result is most likely uninspired workers. On the other hand, being too nice creates an undisciplined structure that tolerates less than ideal performance. Greed and ego are also involved. Good business people need healthy egos to be successful, and they have to have passion for what they do. Greed in small, controlled doses plays into self-motivation, but when ego and greed become the primary drivers in people's career, these people are considered poor team players and less than ideal leadership candidates. The challenge is to balance the management style of the organization with the diverse personalities of the employees and make changes accordingly. Reverting to his gardener mode, Bill draws a parallel to a stagnant pond, "If you do not have fresh water constantly feeding into the pond, the water becomes putrid, all the oxygen is sucked out, and no fish can grow, so fresh water needs to flow in and water needs to flow out to maintain the proper dynamics of a healthy organization."

Do Over?

Bill's response to this question was not one of remorse but one of affirmation. "I know that I am in the right spot in this stage in my life; the only slight regret I have is that I wish I had started my consulting business earlier. To be able to give sound advice based on one's life experiences, one does need some gray hair, but I did not need to be in the corporate world for 30 years to accomplish what I'm doing today." Bill does not guide his future by looking in a rearview mirror, so he has no regrets and feels blessed to have worked in an industry that he loves and in which he can continue help others.

VISION OF THE FUTURE

Bill had always planned to be out of the corporate world by his mid-50s and doing consulting work based on expertise that over the last 30 years he had developed while working for someone else. His philosophy was to work less and live more, so he is right on schedule. He sees great opportunity even in a bad economy and views the service that he offers as being more important than ever.

Today's communication technology with e-mail, twitter, Google alerts, and instant messages amazes Arman. He does not, however, think this replaces face-to-face personal relationship building - with the challenge being to balance the two. Those who figure this out will have a distinct competitive advantage.

Arman considers the green industry to have a great promise for the future. Whether or not they realize it, everyone in the U.S. is impacted by what the professionals of our industry contribute to the communities in which we live. The industry has a positive impact on the environment every day and adds value to peoples' lives and properties.

THE HEAD HARVESTER

Bill signs his correspondence Harvester Bill. As all good gardeners know, it takes four seasons to harvest a crop. It starts in the spring with the performance of the basics required for fruitful planting. These basics include removing roots, rocks, and debris, tilling the soil, and grading the ground. It takes discipline, training, and the right tools and skill sets to achieve the ideal soil conditions for healthy growth and development of plants. It is all about the roots and proper plant selection. If the fundamentals are not correct, the end results are going to be disappointing. Summer is a time of nurturing the plants with tender loving care, weeding, fertilizing, and watering; plus, when necessary, fending off insects and diseases. Equally important, sometimes tough love is necessary to prune, sucker and brace to promote vigorous and healthy growth. In the fall, the rewards of one's work can be seen by all - in the splendor of the foliage and the beauty of the landscape. Winter is for regeneration and sharing the bounty and planning for the coming season. For professional development in the green industry, the same season of events is true. It takes four seasons to fully harvest one's potential.

Fine Wine

Bill Arman is proud of his California roots and even prouder of its wines. He prides himself on his knowledge of viticulture, especially the drinking part. He sometimes enhances his consulting training sessions with tastings of his favorite reds. If one were to compare Bill to a wine, the description might be as follows: a deep bodied cabernet, which to achieve the ultimate sense of temperament has been aged in the finest of oak barrels, highlighted with subtle notes of wit and sage, combined with overtones of humor, and a smooth finish of fun with no hint of bitterness. A fine wine indeed!

SHARON BARNES

Some people are born into a business, some start their own, and some are hired. Sharon Barnes did it the old-fashioned way - she married into it. At the time, her sights were not set on a career in the green industry, but rather on the pursuit of a special-education degree in teaching. She did not start working at the family nursery until after she raised her children. When she did start, it was a process of learning on the job; working from the ground floor up. Today she is recognized as one of the country's leading authorities in source-separated composting. She served several years as the president of the US Composting Council, and currently is president of the Organics Recycling Association of Ohio.

When you meet Sharon Barnes, there are no outward signs that she is a major force in the nursery business and an expert on composting. She has a warm and engaging smile that belies a deep-seated passion and commitment to her family, her business and her chosen profession. She has a calm and seasoned confidence in her abilities that have been strengthened and tempered by the hottest fires. She learned at an early age to be independent and self-reliant.

IN THE BEGINNING

After serving in the European theater in World War II and earning a degree from The Ohio State University on the G.I. Bill, Harold Barnes (Sharon's father-in-law) and his two brothers started Barnes Roses in the early 1950s. Harold had worked with roses while at Wyatt Roses in Northern Ohio. He liked roses and saw a business opportunity, so he moved, along with his brothers to Huron, Ohio to be close to Lake Erie, which had cool summers and long growing seasons that were ideal for rose propagation. In 1957, he bought out his two brothers; this left him with $17 in his pocket and a $100,000 mortgage.

Two more challenges followed. The first was that as much as Harold enjoyed roses, Harold's only son and Sharon's future husband, Robert, hated them. The process of propagation was a difficult, tedious, and sticky ordeal. The second was that the interstate highway system started in the 1950s led to the demise of the once flourishing rose growing business in Northern Ohio. The highways were designed to alleviate congested state roads and facilitate rapid movement of military troops and equipment from one area to another. The actual impacts were, however, much broader and more profound and even affected the green industry. Once the coasts were connected by the new highway system, it was not long before California-grown, bare-rooted roses were showing up in retail outlets nationwide. Like other industries, rose production was transformed by efficient transportation extending the reach of lower-cost producers. This was one of many paradigm shifts that the Barneses have had to deal with in their company's 60-year history.

From Roses to Begonias

By 1969, the decision was made to exit the rose business and concentrate on growing trees, shrubs, and ornamentals. The name of the company was changed to Barnes Nursery. Robert and Sharon were married and graduated from The Ohio State University in horticulture and special-education, respectively. With their young son, Jarret, they returned to Huron. Robert worked full-time with his dad and Sharon settled in teaching elementary school.

Sharon taught for three years, had a daughter, and stayed home to raise her children until they reached junior high. At this point, she decided to join the family business instead of going back to the classroom. Her decision was based on wanting the freedom to work and live a seasonal schedule with her husband. Her first duties were in the retail garden center where she worked with the public. This was a classic case of learning by doing. She observed the people around her - both customers and fellow workers. With an easy laugh, she says that she learned what a Begonia was when a customer asked her where the Begonia section was located. Sharon dutifully found another coworker who showed her where to look. This process was repeated thousands of times over the next several years. Based on her special-education training and experience, Sharon was well aware that there were many ways of learning besides those that are taught in classrooms. Her father-in-law was a stickler for a neat and clean facility. His philosophy was that when a customer visits your store, it is like visiting your home. The front glass door must be spotless, and the parking lot free of debris, including cigarette butts. Sharon got her share of cleaning windows, toilets, and the parking lot.

Even though Sharon was married to one of the bosses, she always worked for someone else. She never wanted to be a manager but was always engaged in learning the business and operational processes. She worked hard at her job. As the company grew, the garden center became an ever more important portal for the landscaping side of the business. Here, Sharon began helping people with small landscape projects, so she naturally evolved from the retail into horticultural-services side. From the 1970s through the 1990s, by branching out into lawncare and landscaping, the company enjoyed strong growth and, in the process, built a strong team of managers and loyal workers. During the second half of the 1990s, sales doubled in just five years. This outpaced the Barneses' administrative abilities to control costs and maintain profits. Sales may have doubled, but the profits were shrinking. The next paradigm shift was about to occur.

Compost Happened

As a consequence of the rapid growth of the landscaping business, yard waste began to accumulate at the Barnes Nursery dumpsite, which was close to a major road. Unbeknownst to the Barneses, an employee was dumping personal trash with the yard waste. When a particularly strong windstorm occurred, trash was spread over the road. Complaints were made; the city inspected the site and identified the culprit. In turn, restrictions permitted only yard waste to be stored.

At this point, Sharon started researching composting as a possible solution to the ever-increasing mounds of yard waste. She thought that composting could be developed into a new business and was given the go-ahead to develop a business plan. She decided to seek guidance by contacting people by phone; her first call was to Dr. Eldon Smith, her former horticulture professor (she had taken some horticulture courses as electives). She received her best advice on this initial call when Dr. Smith said, "If you go into composting, your objective should be to only make a top product that can be used as a high-end horticulture amendment." He went on to explain that people had failed to commercialize composting because they focused on getting rid of waste. This approach produced poor-quality finished products, for which there was no market. To learn the fundamentals and best techniques for producing high quality compost, Sharon called Dr. Harry Hoytink of the Ohio Agriculture Research and Development Center. To produce high quality compost, she learned that one had to start with high quality, source separated materials. Non-green wastes such as garbage and industrial by-products could not be included, unless specifically qualified and treated in a special manner.

The green movement began in the 1990s, during which time the nation was running out of landfill space and there was a focus on recycling. Due to rising perceptions and criticisms that disposable baby diapers were filling landfills at an alarming rate, Procter & Gamble got involved with composting research and donated $20 million to create the Solid Waste Composting Council. Sharon joined the Council to gain more information from leaders in the field but soon found herself in a leadership position. After several years, when the research support was coming to an end, a group of organic composters formed the US Composting Council, and Sharon became its first president. Funding was tight, but Sharon devoted her full-time attention to righting the ship and paving the path to hire a full-time professional executive director. She was able to do this because of her great staff support at the nursery. Sharon made site visits throughout the country and was invited twice to Japan to work with Japan's composting association. During this period, she became involved with the Organics Recycling Association of Ohio and as of this writing is its president.

Being at the forefront of a national trade association, Sharon had a steep learning curve. It was a big step to move from practically no managerial responsibility to being the leader of a large, volunteer association with more than 1,000 members. She learned early that regardless of the group's size, few people were willing to take on responsibilities, so she and a small group did the heavy lifting of running the organization. A phenomenon she observed was that with bigger member companies there were continual personnel shifts that made it difficult to get a decision. It was a frustrating and tiring experience.

Another lesson she carried forward is that when you are trying to sell or asking for support for a product or program, you should never cry "poor." You must always put your best foot forward and even if your clothes are old and you have fear in your heart - you make sure your clothes are pressed and cleaned and put on your best face. You put a smile on your face and remember the power of perception and attitude. If people perceive you as a professional, you have credibility and trust.

PROBLEM SOLVING

Sharon admits to having a unique process for learning and solving problems. She is a people watcher, and she pays special attention to those she admires the most. She watches and studies their reactions to successes and tragedies, and she tries to model her behavior to the best qualities she has observed in others. She adopted this learning style in elementary school and has practiced it her whole life.

Do Over

When asked if given the chance, what she would do over, Sharon quickly responded,

> Funny you should ask; I was just thinking about this the other night. When I grew up in the 1950s and '60s, women's opportunities were limited to basically three careers--nursing, teaching, or secretarial, so I chose teaching. Knowing what I know today, I would have majored in business with a focus on administrative management and made business a career.

She does think her education training and working with special education children helped her work with people from different walks of life, but she also thinks that she could have brought special insights into her family business if she had earlier business training.

I Knew I Had Made It When.....

"I had the grace to come to grips with the past of a very negative experience." It was a surprising statement from a successful businesswoman who sits on numerous committees and boards and is a national composting leader. No mention was made of help growing Barnes Nursery to over $10 million in sales or heading up one of the largest composting associations in the world. Rather it was the aftermath of surviving a difficult and nasty battle with what she termed "environmental terrorists" who unfairly targeted Barnes and misrepresented facts regarding a marsh that was part of their private property.

The Army Corps of Engineers had approved an application by Barnes to tap part of a marsh for water for their nursery, but once a local environmental group became aware of the permit, they made life a living hell with false allegations that forced the EPA and the state Attorney General's office into the dispute. Even with experts testifying that there would be no harm, the negative publicity forced the Corps to rescind their approval. After a long, drawn out battle, Barnes withdrew its request.

This was a bitter pill, but Sharon admits that she came out stronger and better because of the experience. She said that they took the high road at all times and held their heads high even though the other side was ignorant and vicious. Barnes navigated the tough times with class, and it helped her define who she is. The experience gave her confidence for the future. "You have to take the horrible experiences in stride knowing that they, too, will pass, and use them as learning experiences." Sharon knew she had made it when she came through this adversity with her integrity intact. Even though she lost her case, she was able to move on and find other alternatives to fill the nursery's water needs.

This lesson was applied again years later when ground that Barnes was leasing for growing nursery stock passed through inheritance to new owners. Even though the heirs were receiving a fair price ($800 per acre) for land in the area, the heirs assumed that because Barnes had established nursery stock planted in the ground, they could blackmail Barnes into paying higher rent. They were wrong on two fronts: first they overestimated the rental value of the land and second they underestimated the resolve of a family that had been in the nursery business for over 50 years. After negotiations went nowhere, Barnes simply bulldozed the stock and returned the land to the heirs.

THE FINAL PARADIGM SHIFT

Ultimately, the transformation of Sharon Barnes's career has been the biggest and most important paradigm shift for Barnes Nursery. Paradigm is defined as a generally accepted model of how ideas relate to one another. When Sharon was initially choosing her career; her choices were limited to being a nurse, a secretary or teacher. Around this same time, the women's movement was gathering momentum. Although Sharon was not following the same path as the protesters being seen on nightly TV, she arrived at the same destination. She did it against all odds, with no formal business or even technical training. She was a woman in a man's world and a pioneer in every sense of the word.

Definition of a Professional

Sharon defines professionals as people who are passionate about what they do, have uncompromising standards, care for their people and their communities, and most important, they measure their successes by these same criteria. When asked whether she considers herself a professional, she modestly responded, "I hope I am," and added, "I think so." Yes, Sharon, you are the definition of a professional.

A Lady for All Seasons

When Sharon was a little girl she patterned herself after those she admired. We would all do ourselves proud if we followed Sharon's lead and modeled our behavior after hers.

JOHN GIBSON

The office is not indicative of a person who is president of an $18 million company. It is not a bit ostentatious no plaques - no awards - just a nondescript space situated among other nondescript spaces down the corridor. Its only distinguishing characteristic seemed to be its location: a mere 15 feet from the back exit. The office reflects the modest personality of the occupant who during off time hunts big game in the Rockies and during meetings gets to the point and kicks elephants.

At the age of 40, John Gibson was named president of Swingle Lawn, Tree & Landscape Care (one of the largest lawncare and tree companies in the U.S.). His journey to the top was not as linear as one might suspect. Along the way, there were several detours, which he likes to refer to as learning experiences. He calls his 18-year affiliation, almost half of his life span, with various professional associations and 22 years in the green industry as a training ground for navigating around the detours and developing and honing his leadership and managerial skills.

Fear and Intimidation

John's first job in the industry was as a mowing-crew foreman. His management style, he admits, was one of fear and intimidation. After all, his role models were his football coaches in high school and college. During this period John played fullback on a semi-pro football team, so during the day he mowed grass, and at nightfall mowed down the competition by donning shoulder pads and helmet. In college, Gibson was an all-conference fullback and punter.

Football is a physical contact sport with the success of the team depending upon players executing assignments in disciplined manners. There is little room for improvising that occurs in basketball and soccer because it is absolutely crucial for all players to be team players and bend their wills to benefit the team. Coaches are dictators who make this happen.

At least that was John's experience during his high school and college football days. This was not the case, however, when he played semi-pro football. The word "semi" meant that players were not paid; therefore, money was not a motivator just as their scream-in-your-face coach was not a motivator. The coach allowed the African-American players to practice self-imposed segregation and warm up separately from the rest of the team. Because all the running backs for whom John blocked were African-Americans, John asked the group to join him in practice to iron out some plays. His request was denied. Primarily responsible for blocking and opening up holes in the line, John needed to work on timing with his running back counterparts, but first he needed to get their attention. John said, "That was easy. The first play from scrimmage, I simply stepped aside and allowed a middle linebacker to come rushing through untouched to crush the running back. After that experience, I no longer had to coax my fellow players to practice as a team."

Team First

In sports and in business, teamwork is paramount. Your success as a player or as an entrepreneur depends on those around you. Since his football playing days, John's leadership style has mellowed like a fine bourbon whiskey. He still has plenty of character and is full-bodied, but now he has a broader understanding of other peoples' feelings, motivations, and capabilities. He credits his boss and mentor, company owner Tom Tolkacz, and his experience as PLANET's second president with helping him create his management style. John understands that to be a successful leader he "needs to be in the other person's map of the world." It is less about fear and intimidation and more about being attentive to the human side of the equation.

For the last several years, to help understand the makeup of its leadership team, Swingle Tree and Lawncare has used personality testing, which John thinks is an excellent tool when used properly. "It can be especially helpful for areas in which understanding personality traits can help resolve conflicts, improve communications, and balance teams." He, however, warns against the temptation to pigeonhole individuals because of their personality test results. A person identified by testing to be an introvert may possess great technical knowledge, have a natural ability to gain client trust, be able to build relationships, and therefore be a top salesperson.

John also cautions against selecting team players in your own image. As he explains, one has to fight this tendency in order to ensure team balance. "If team members have the same educational backgrounds, took the same subjects in school, attended the same schools, read the same books and had the same grades, they would be a direct reflection of each other and ultimately of yourself. When this dynamic occurs, and it often does, someone or everyone is ultimately redundant."

GOAL ORIENTED

In his early life, John admits to being short-term goal oriented. "Get the lawn mowed, make a first down - that was my focus. I was achieving specific goals and not looking very far into the future." He has now moved from being focused on goals to enjoying the experience of the journey. By stepping back from merely trying to make it to the next stop on the line, John has found an appreciation for finding the meaning within the trip.

Because of his different experiences, John thinks he is prepared for whatever the future brings, and he has a sense that there will be larger, different opportunities down the road. He is optimistic about our industry and thinks the economy will bounce back although there will be challenges, especially finding enough labor to handle pent-up demands for services.

His biggest success is that he has always had the courage to develop people under him to take his place. This, in turn, has allowed him to grow. John is proud of his volunteer-leadership experience during which he learned to understand his role in various positions and to look at the big picture instead of "What's in it for me." He takes his greatest pride, though, in knowing that he is leaving behind a living legacy in the people who have learned from his mentoring and who follow in his footsteps.

JERRY GROSSI

Jerry Grossi came into the green industry by the back door. While at Michigan State University, Jerry studied to be a high school teacher; however, by graduation, his dream to be a teacher had faded. His first job was with Blue Cross Blue Shield. This experience did not excite Jerry any more than being a science teacher, so he took a job with Spartan Maintenance, which specialized in cleaning and maintaining buildings. On the weekends, he would team up with a Michigan State University fraternity brother who had a side business of promoting rock concerts in the area. This business venture eventually failed, but Jerry found a business partner for life in Ed Dudgeon. Ed was an Ohio farm boy who was butting heads with his father over farming the same piece of dirt, so Ed joined Jerry at Spartan Maintenance where they eventually bought the owner out and began expanding into exterior maintenance. Their business was incorporated on April 1, 1976 and to this day is a partnership is built on sharing work and trusting each other.

From Condominiums to Trees

In the beginning, their business focused on serving condominium complexes with mowing, lawncare, snow removal, and building maintenance. This eventually evolved into comprehensive property management that included dealing with owners associations. Management was Ed's specialty while Jerry's was development of the lawncare, irrigation, and exterior maintenance side of the business. In 1984, they purchased Arbor Lawn, which was their entry into the residential lawncare market. Today Ed continues to run the condo management business while Jerry runs the outdoor business. On the exterior side, irrigation delivers twice as much as lawncare revenues. Several years ago, Christmas Decor was added as a business unit, which Jerry reports has good synergy with their clients and market demographics. Christmas Decor replaced snowplowing as a revenue source and has proven to be preferable from a management and labor perspective.

Profile of a Successful Partnership

To start their business, Jerry and Ed put in equal amounts of their own money. They even shared the same living quarters to save money. In 1978, they took out loans to fund their growth ambitions. This fueled their rapid expansion in the 1980s. They were well on their way by the early 1980s when the interest rate crisis occurred. Marginal rates by that time were 12 to 14% - if you could even get a loan. This was followed by the fuel crisis, which caused restrictions on refueling and long lines at every gas station. Eventually interest rates peaked at 21%. Fortunately, both Jerry and Ed thought that managing with a strong balance sheet was wise, so they were able to pay off their loans as their interest rates skyrocketed. Jerry recalls that during this period the companies that grew quickly on borrowed money died the same way.

Finally the challenges of the 1980s faded and gave way to the boom of the 1990s. This was before Hispanic workers and H-2B workers, so finding employees to work at green-industry wages was difficult. Demand for labor was so high that the building trades and manufacturers were now taking the usual pool of workers. The number of college students willing to work in labor-intensive jobs for entry-level wages also disappeared as their interests shifted to career oriented internships or taking summers off.

By the beginning of 2000, the boom was over in Michigan, especially in Detroit. This downturn started five to six years before the rest of the country, and what started out as a recession has now evolved into what many are calling a civic collapse. This gave Jerry a head start in dealing with challenging economic situations. He and Ed learned quickly that they had to work even harder and selling became more difficult. During this time, a mantra in their office was "When the economy recovers...." (that is, they would be able to do this or that). It is now uncertain if that the local economy is ever going to recover back to its former self.

Association Man for All Seasons

Jerry's association experience started with the Michigan Lawn Sprayers Association, which was based in Detroit and had approximately 70 small operators as members. One of the first meetings that Jerry attended was on developing the Association's bylaws. Given Jerry's condo management experience, he was widely versed on bylaws. He did such a good job that he was elected president and was later elected to the Michigan Turfgrass Foundation that had approximately 1,800 members. He served as president for two years and was on the board of directors nine years. Through this organization, Jerry became familiar with the Professional Land Care Association of America and attended his first "Day on the Hill" in 1984 as an allied regional committee representative. This ultimately led to Jerry being elected to the Board of Directors and then president of PLCAA. As a result, over the last 20 years, Jerry has continually been either a director or president of numerous green-industry associations. Jerry has made major contributions to the Green Industry Expo and now the GIE/Expo tradeshow. No other industry volunteer has more experience or done more to ensure the success of the trade show than Jerry Grossi. He is presently serving on the Board of Directors of PLANET as president-elect.

Passions

It is obvious from Jerry's volunteer work with green-industry trade associations that he has a passion for our profession. He has always had a desire to be successful and has had a similar wish for those around him. Jerry's company has many long-term employees - some have worked for the company for more than 20 years - and he wants them, as well as himself, to be part of a respected industry. He is a man of his word and does not make commitments casually. His 33-year partnership and 20+year volunteer record are grand testimonies to his commitment and dedication to his beliefs.

Jerry is proud of his family. He enjoys helping his children and grandchildren and makes time for his family. There are no family members involved in the business at this time.

You Know You've Made it, When...

You start building a team to achieve a company vision and goals. This occurred in the early 1980s when Jerry and his partner Ed Dudgeon inked a multifaceted property management and maintenance contract. The contract included several large office complexes. The scope of the work covered all aspects of property care and management, excluding leasing. This enabled them to enlarge their staff by over 30 people. It provided an anchor and a base of operations to develop middle-level management and springboard into the lawncare and irrigation businesses, which are core businesses today.

Skill Sets

Jerry describes himself as a logical person with a tendency to sometimes be too analytical. He is proud of his ability to be a consensus builder and prefers to build and function in a team rather than being a dictator. Jerry possesses uncanny common sense, along with an even disposition, which allows him to think before he reacts.

Keys to Success

The keys to long-term success are developing people to work well in a team structure and developing a strong middle management staff that requires minimal direct supervision. This is achieved by giving people the opportunities to grow each and every day.

SUCCESS DEFINED

At this stage of life, Jerry does not define success with money. He defines success as the personal gratification of building something larger than yourself and being happy with yourself and your organization. Success is sometimes defined by the extent to which you have achieved your childhood expectations/goals. Jerry always wanted to be in management and to be his own person and boss. He aspired to be neither a lawyer nor a doctor; rather his preference was to be a leader in the business world. By this definition Jerry is a successful, self-made man.

Growing up, Jerry was never without a job. His dad was one of the original employees of Kelly Office Services. Jerry had his pick of temporary jobs; or, more accurately, his father had his pick of temporary jobs for Jerry. "I worked all the time." Weekends, holidays, and, without question, summers were opportunities for employment. "If I came home from college for the weekend, my dad had a day job for me for both Saturday and Sunday. I worked every odd job that you can imagine from janitor, office helper, inventory taker, to messenger. It was great on-the-job training." This early experience and exposure to the business world has served Jerry well in both his business and association work.

DO OVER

When asked what Jerry would do over if given the opportunity, he immediately replied that the largest mistake he and Ed made was not thinking big enough. Early on, their mindset was diversifying into too many business segments and not focusing on what their core strengths should be. The net result was that they were a transactional business in the process of developing relationships; there were too many small projects and not enough attention on endeavors that would allow them to grow. Looking back, if they had focused more on expanding their lawncare services geographically they would be a larger company today. Chasing too many opportunities restricted their growth and strained their managerial and financial resources.

Stagnant Sales Equal Stale Employees

Due to a decreasing revenue stream, promotions and raises are becoming difficult to fund. Good, long-term employees are basically running in place. In a depressed market, the challenge is to keep employees mentally and physically on-the-job and motivated. Doing this takes creativity and leadership based on trust and transparency.

Vision for the Future

Jerry sees a positive future for the green industry. He believes the demand for services will continue to grow as more people realize that green spaces increase the quality of lives. Along the way, there will be challenges with regard to environmental, governmental, regulatory, and public perception issues. Jerry strongly believes as members of the green industry the benefits of green spaces must be promoted to counter negative perceptions. He points out that the market wants services provided by the green industry and this fact needs to be leveraged to help raise awareness.

Personal Vision

Jerry plans staying on the job through his 60s and is presently working to transition his staff to take on more responsibility and control. His succession plan is a 10-year process.

ROBERT HAYTER

Robert Hayter is a product of Appalachia. He was born and raised in southwestern Virginia, and his roots there run deep. Prior to the Revolutionary War, his ancestors migrated from England, and the name Hayter means "keeper of the hay," a most appropriate name for someone who ultimately made a career in the green industry. Robert's father was a truck driver who passed away when Robert was 16 years old, and his mother was a waitress. From this humble beginning, Robert graduated from high school, spent a brief period during the Vietnam War in the military, and obtained a two-year degree from Sandhills Community College, in Pinehurst, North Carolina. With this background, he ventured into the wide world of business.

EARLY ENTREPRENEUR SPIRIT

In 1959, at nine years of age, Robert purchased a lawn mower from the local Pep Boys store and began mowing lawns. This was his introduction to the green industry, and it became a career path for the rest of his life. Robert, while in high school, had a part-time job with the Virginia Department of Transportation Test lab where he developed an interest in soils. He always had a fascination with gardens, and, when a work colleague suggested that he attend Sandhills Community College in North Carolina, he enrolled there after his military service. Robert received a two-year associate's degree in Landscape Gardening. His first job after graduation was with the notable North Carolina entrepreneur Walter Davis, for whom he was responsible for developing the Public Master Plan for a 30-acre property fronting the Pasquotank River. The property included a personal estate, a residential development, and extensive gardens. His next employment was with Waynesboro Landscape and Nursery as an assistant retail manager.

Instructor/Student/ Entrepreneur - the Renaissance Years

In 1974, Robert returned to Sandhills CC as an instructor in arboriculture, nursery trades, and landscape design and construction. For the next 13 years, he instructed students in the field or in the classroom and was also a student himself, earning a BS in Horticultural Science and a Masters of Agriculture from North Carolina State University. During his entire academic career, he was in a constant teaching and learning mode, and, as he advanced in the teaching ranks and his college level studies, he developed a wide and large number of influential friends who were either mentors or mentees. Ironically, while he was working on his undergraduate and advanced degrees, many of his students were four-year graduates from prestigious universities. These graduates were attending Sandhills to build career paths. This is where Robert developed a passion for learning and sharing his knowledge with his students. He became in his own words a "student of life" and realized he was happiest when he is constantly learning.

Robert credits the late J. C. Raulston of North Carolina State University as being a major influence on his personal as well as his professional life. Dr. Raulston helped Robert focus his wide range of interests, discipline his education track, and hone his teaching skills. Robert relates that the only argument he ever had with Professor Raulston was when he decided not to pursue a Ph.D. degree because he did not want to narrow his focus. He wanted to be more of a generalist rather than a specialist. During this 13-year period, Robert re-engaged his entrepreneurial spirit on the family farm by starting a wholesale nursery business. Through self-study, he also became a registered Landscape Architect in North Carolina and Virginia. Robert describes this time as an important journey motivated by the desire to obtain knowledge and a better understanding on how to build and maintain natural environments.

From Mowing Lawns in Virginia to Building Fantasy Landscapes in Paradise

Most green industry professionals take a lifetime to achieve total accumulative sales of $7 million, let alone achieving this spectacular volume in their first couple of years of operation, but when Robert started his landscape design and installation business after the approval of his first contract, this is exactly what happened. This is the same pattern of events that occurred with his other successful, green-industry professions: become an instructor and simultaneously work on a college degree, land a multimillion landscape construction job and build the company to accomplish the work. First visualizing the end results and then plot the paths to achieve your goals.

Sometimes perfect alignments of times, places, and people occur and these change the courses of peoples' lives and careers. The events and factors that come together may be serendipitous, but they are not pure luck, particularly for people such as Robert who worked hard to be a renaissance professional in the green industry. When at a cocktail party, Robert's insular world of southeastern landscape design and teaching was knocked out of orbit when he met a broker who worked for a European business consortium that was planning to build a resort on the Caribbean island of Antigua, West Indies. He asked Robert if he would be interested in the lead landscape architect position. When Robert responded positively, he soon found himself sitting across the table from the Prime Minister of Antigua. At the completion of the meeting, the contract was his. As part of the contract, it was agreed that Robert would retain his position at Sandhills Community College and would spend a week of every month on the site.

The President of the College was thrilled that someone from the faculty had received international recognition, as it would bring prestige to the school. This was not, however, the case with the other professors and instructors. Due to jealousy and envy, they protested this was not fair and argued it was not in the best interest of the college to have a part-time, globetrotting instructor on staff. Yielding to peer pressure, Robert made a decision that changed his career path forever; he resigned his professorship. Ultimately, this turned out to be the right decision, for when he started the planning stages of the project, he quickly realized that because the project was being funded by a consortium of German and Dutch banks and managed from Europe, the traditional operational mode for the lead landscape architect in that environment was "you design it, you build it." He was given an almost unlimited budget and total authority over the execution of the work. With this total responsibility came total accountability. It was good that Robert was a fast learner and that the many years he had spent in the academic and business worlds had prepared him for this great adventure.

It was also good that Robert was a little naïve with regard to the magnitude of the project he was undertaking. He assembled a great team, and, most important he hired a former military officer who was experienced in materials logistics. As part of Robert's responsibilities, he approved and contracted for all the soft and hard goods plus made the payments. During the height of the project, the interest on the overnight deposits from Europe that were used to pay the daily invoices were larger than Robert's fees. With all this responsibility and activity swirling around, Robert realized that he could not be a player in the band; he had to be the leader of the band. He learned to delegate and trust in his employees and great things happened. Based on the success Robert was having, halfway through this project, he was asked by the Italian designer, Krizia Mandelli, to design and build the landscape for a private resort on Barbuda, a small island attached to Antigua, W. I. As construction from the first project started to close down, Robert was working at full speed to design and install the landscape for the now famous K Club Resort in Barbuda. Just as the influx of European money from Arab-oil wealth started to wind down, Robert completed a third Caribbean project.

FROM PARADISE TO HISTORICAL LANDMARKS

After four years of concentrated effort in the Caribbean, Robert turned his attention to consulting, and focused his landscape architectural firm on providing services for traditional resorts, garden centers, and landscape facilities. This brought him into contact with such prestigious places as Williamsburg, The Homestead in Hot Springs, Virginia, and The Mount Washington Resort in Brettonwoods, New Hampshire. Closer to home he became the resident landscape architect for The Pinehurst Resort, and, in 1999 and 2005, he was the event landscape architect for the U.S. Open Golf Championship.

As Robert moved away from large, design-build projects to working with historical landscape sites, he discovered that he had to employ a new skill set. The challenge was to make improvements and upgrades to the properties' original designs and installations, yet make it appear that nothing had been changed. This is an art form that cannot be taught in classrooms. It is more of an intuitive process requiring a keen ability to visualize in three dimensions. Here again, he employed his ability to picture the desired end result and work to achieve it. He did this to make the Mount Washington Resort, which was built in 1902, more competitive and user friendly. Although the Hotel, which was located in the White Mountains of New Hampshire, was beautiful and unique, the building's relationship to the landscape was awkward and did not feature the best aspects of its beauty and uniqueness. After 104 years, this "strangeness" was accepted as part of the mystique of Mount Washington, but this "strangeness" was creating major traffic flow problems. Robert sensed that something was wrong on his first visit, but it was not until he and his team walked the property from the front gate to the entrance of the hotel that it dawned on them that the original driveway must have been built for vehicles to be driven on the left side of the road. A little investigation confirmed that at the beginning of the 20th Century, after the English model, locally built horseless carriages had their steering wheels on their right sides and the road had been built to accommodate local vehicles.

The solution to the problem was to redesign the approach so that modern cars could approach the hotel as originally intended by directing traffic in the opposite direction; maybe a simple solution, but it took a little over a century to figure out.

Another example is the Homestead, a popular high-end destination on the East Coast. The hotel is a luxury facility located in the heart of the Virginia Allegheny Mountains. Over the years a common quote of the guests was "You can look out of the building but you cannot get out of it." The problem was that there were not adequate exit points on the backside of the hotel to access the landscaping and gardens. This challenge was solved by creating a landscape design that integrated steps to a new rear entrance. This elegant solution changed the function of the property but not its overall ambiance. Returning guests swore that the rear entrance had always been there and nothing had been changed. To Robert, this is the highest level of compliment. Here again, Robert had the ability to visualize in his mind the desired outcome and execute the design and installation to fit his mental image.

Favorite Success Story

When asked what his favorite success story is, Robert does not list any of his projects or accomplishments; rather he suggests there is parallel between his career and that of the incredible 1803-to-1806 journey of discovery made by Meriwether Lewis and William Clark. Robert's philosophy is that the journey is more important than the pursuit of an end product. When asked when he knew that he had made it, he said, "I have not reached that goal, because I never set a goal to be a success at any one thing." He considers each accomplishment as a stepping-stone that allows him to take on and succeed in his next adventure. He is motivated by playing the game more than the scorecard. Doing good work ensures that there will always be another assignment. He never wants to be told he cannot play the game.

LESSONS LEARNED

Robert has few regrets, but one has to do with his investments in real estate. He got caught up in speculative projects because he thought there were opportunities, but, in reality, there were not any. In retrospect, he relied too much on emotion and face value without having objective proofs to justify his investments. He admits this may be a trait from childhood - in some cases he is too trusting. These setbacks may have caused financial hits, but they have not dampened his spirit and optimism for the future.

THE FUTURE

At this stage of his life, Robert is focusing on becoming a counselor of value for small to mid-range companies in the green industry. His greatest job satisfaction comes from being involved with and having positive impacts on other peoples' lives. He has a passion for sharing his knowledge with others and learning from those whom he is counseling. To help companies recognize and improve their limitations, he has created a program he has named Optimum Provision Management (OPM). His OPM program has been widely accepted by a group of upper-end landscape companies in North Carolina. Based on this success, Robert plans to expand this program nationally.

He thinks that the sustainability movement is a noble future responsibility of the green industry. Gone are the vast forests that used to cover the Eastern and Midwestern United States. The numbers and sizes of family farms have also diminished. Urban landscapes are becoming the dominant environment, so it is important that landscapers and lawncare operators transition to more sustainable practices and become stewards of the green environments where people live. Robert wants to be a leader in this movement.

His view is that many green industry companies and the industry in general are at maturation stages, as most of its products and services are being commoditized. The industry needs to find a way to communicate to the general public that the contributions made by the green industry go beyond the beauty and aesthetics of green spaces. A focus should be put on the natural assets and positive benefits that lawns, gardens, and trees are to our planet's ecosystem. There is a high level need to monetize/quantify these benefits. The costs of removing trees and landscapes from our planet's ecosystem should be documented in terms that the general public can understand.

"Master of the Hay"

In summing up Robert Hayter's career, it is safe to say that he has lived up to his ancestral name and even stepped it up a notch or two from the "keeper of the hay" to the "Master of the Hay."

JENNIFER LEMCKE

Although Jennifer was not born into the lawncare business, her first job, at age 12, was as a telemarketer for her next-door neighbor who owned a Weed Man lawncare franchise. Because she could not take the constant rejections, as it was too much for her pre-teen psyche to handle, she only lasted five days. From this early experience of working a multitude of jobs through high school and college, she did not give lawncare another thought.

A Family Affair

Jen was born into a family with a rich business and entrepreneurial bloodline. Her mother's family operated Canadian Tire retail outlets, and her father was a rising corporate executive. While in college, Jennifer found she had a knack for systems and computers and eventually found a job working for Ottawa University in the telecommunications department as a coordinator for electronic education.

Tiring of corporate life, Jennifer's father Roger Mongeon became fascinated with the success of the Weed Man lawncare operation of his neighbor (yes, the same neighbor who gave Jen her first job), so Roger traded in his executive pinstripe suits for the uniform of a Weed Man franchise owner, and he opened the first Weed Man franchise in Hull, Québec. Based on the success of his first Weed Man operation, he opened a second franchise in Montreal, Québec. Roger set his eyes on expanding into the Ontario marketplace and invited Jennifer to join him as a management trainee. Here she learned every aspect of the lawncare business from running the call center (a full 360 degrees back to her first job but this time she lasted over five years) to pulling hoses on client's lawns. Her husband joined Jennifer to manage a second franchise in Ottawa, where they rapidly grew the business to over $2 million in six years.

Based on this success, her father asked Jennifer to become the office manager of the Toronto headquarters to help develop and implement a new software program for office administration. This required Jennifer to hit the road and train the various operations on how to use the new software and to implement standard operating procedures in each of the branch offices. This was done while she was also raising a family.

This double and even triple tasking forced Jennifer to develop a focused work ethic and a world-class education in the intricacies of managing a lawncare operation. It was possible because she had worked at every level in the business from worker, supervisor, and manager to executive. Simply put, she climbed the ladder to the top by doing every job at every step, and it all was done under the watchful eye of her father and mentor. By 2000, it was almost preordained for Jennifer's father to again tap his daughter on the shoulder and offer her the position of COO of Turf Holdings, Inc., owner of the franchise rights to the Weed Man name in the United States.

The Pay Off

From the tears of a frustrated, 12-year-old, rejected telemarketer to the head of Weed Man USA, the payoff from all the years of hard work was impressive. In her first year, in an already saturated lawncare market, she helped bring in seven sub-franchises, which represented 28 franchise operations. This was quite an accomplishment for someone in her 30s and a female in a mostly male-dominated industry.

When you meet Jennifer, the first thing you notice is her warm and genuine smile. This is reinforced with a friendly personality that seems to be a birthright of those born north of the border. When you talk to her, a persona of calm confidence becomes readily apparent. Once you get to know her, it is apparent that if you were choosing team members to run your business operations; she would be a first-round draft choice.

An important aspect of Jennifer's career development is that early on she wanted to be independent. She always worked and held a multitude of jobs. She thought she had found her niche in the Otawa University telecommunications department, a job that she found challenging and rewarding, but by the age of 23, like a compass needle always returning to magnetic north, her genetic roots triggered the entrepreneurial bug. Thus, her independence phase morphed into a desire to be a part of the family business not only with her father, but also with her husband Chris. For the equivalent of three dollars an hour, she traded in the intellectual and highly organized world of managing electrons to an entry-level apprenticeship in a start-up, lawncare operation. This was not a fairy tale princess story in which the father appoints his daughter, the princess heir apparent to become queen; this was more like Cinderella without the wicked stepsisters. No shortcuts, entitlements, nor privileges were given or taken; they were earned by hard work and long hours. Even equity in the new holding company had to be purchased by securing bank loans. Jennifer's dad did not play favorites and was strongly anti-nepotism. This is how a strong family business is built and maintained over multi-generations. Each family member learns the business from the ground floor up, and everyone contributes and earns his or her own keep.

When Jennifer was asked what she thinks her strongest skill set is, she replied, "My frame of mind." She explained she never looks at any problem as being insurmountable. With her strong sense of positive thinking and a conviction in her abilities, she works for a win in all situations. "This is my best asset. I always know there is a solution somewhere." Because of her deep and broad experience base (she has done it all from finance to human relations, sales to production, and entry level to leadership at the highest level), she can quickly analyze, cut out the noise with a keen sense of what is right and fair, and achieve a win-win for both parties. She does admit to becoming angry with people who either prevent or stand in the way of a successful solution.

Caring and Sharing

For all of Jen's business and association accomplishments, and in spite of her hectic work schedule, her top priority is her family. Her three children, Jessica, Justin, and Joshua, are each special in their own rights, combining academic and sports at the highest levels. Her father is her mentor, role model and when needed, a best friend. Jennifer has a perfect circle of love and support.

Jennifer's enthusiasm for sharing and caring does not stop with her family or with her Weed Man colleagues. She is passionate about the green industry and gives unselfishly of her time and experience - even to her competitors!

Although Jennifer is the COO of one of the largest lawncare franchise owners in the U.S., she never mentioned dollars or profits in our conversations. This defines her priorities; her focus is on building relationships, problem solving, and building something larger than the sum of the parts. She looks to the future with optimism but with a sage understanding that major changes are coming. She thinks the green movement will cause a major shift for landscape contractors and lawncare operators. She advises that everyone is going to have to work hard to adapt to these mega-trends and focus energy on becoming leaders, not followers, of sustainability principles and practices. She foresees the world of small businesses will change in a dramatic manner. New regulations are going to have major impacts on labor laws, health care, and environmental issues. She predicts there will be a perfect storm of legislative and regulatory activism. If the green industry does not find a way to work together in dealing with these issues, it will be a splintered voice and will have minimal impact relative to its positions and interests. Based on her Canadian experiences, she has a clear vision of things to come. This is where she thinks trade associations such as PLANET can be most helpful.

Jennifer likes being involved with changes, high-level discussions, productive teams, and making differences. Her style is to be a coach and an instructor. She thinks that her biggest and most important impact is through others. She loves working with her employees and colleagues.

FROM TEARS TO CHEERS

One of Jennifer's favorite stories occurred when she was in her first year of running a tele-communications sales room. By the time she was responsible for the sales room, she could train anybody to be a closer, as long as the person had the right attitude. One lady, however, represented a challenge. Even with repeated training and rehearsal of her sales script, this person could not close a sale. This went on for several nights in a row, each evening ending with the lady in tears. Jennifer again sat down with her and walked her through the correct procedure. The next phone call, the lady made her first sale and was so overwhelmed with her accomplishment that she leaped from her chair, shouted a war whoop, and with tears streaming down her face gave Jennifer a bear hug and said, "This sale was for you." The lady confessed that she was so nervous at not being able to close a sale she was afraid that she was going to be fired. She also said that she would never forget the patience and support that Jennifer gave her - a fitting legacy for the 12-year-old girl who quit her first telemarketing job in tears.

LANDON REEVE

After being in business forty-one years, surviving three recessions, and building a multi-million-dollar operation, Landon Reeve knows what it takes to grow a successful company. Throughout his life, this green industry giant has had a passion for growing things: family, plants, people, and his business. Founder of Maryland-based Chapel Valley Landscape, Landon is a pioneer. When he started his company, there were few landscapers, no mentors, nor strong trade associations. This entrepreneur had no partner with which to bounce ideas and no friendly banker to fund his new enterprise. "I had to fund my business on sweat equity and learn by the seat of my pants."

Early Start

As a teenager, Landon started in the industry by working part-time for four years at a local perennial nursery where he learned from the owner and developed an interest in plants. Because of this experience, he decided to attend the University of Maryland where he majored in ornamental horticulture. After graduating, he returned to the nursery business for a short time before starting his own company in 1968. Looking back over four decades, Landon says those early years could have been smoother if he had only ignored the sirens of growth. Landon explained,

> Back then, business growth was more like climbing stairs than ascending a ramp. Each step represented a new plateau. The fundamentals were basically the same at each level, but the rules changed because of increased sales. New clients led to more complex projects, which, in turn, required hiring new employees with different talent and experience levels. I intuitively understood that a successful business was built on quality work and quality people and that carried the day for us. Yet,

> I could have experienced less stress and chaos if I had more wisely managed growth and profits, which created cash flow issues. Twenty percent annual growth during those early go-go years created serious organizational challenges for our company, challenges that could have been avoided if we had more effectively managed growth.

This is an important lesson for companies transitioning from the start-up to the growth phase and even those that are firmly in the growth phase. How much growth is good and at what point is too much growth an actual deterrent to sustainable business practices? Owners have to answer these questions themselves, but if Landon had it do over, he would have controlled growth and focused more on increasing profitability.

Creating a Culture

Today, Chapel Valley employs upwards of 400 people and has the reputation of being a tremendous training ground for career-minded individuals and having a well-defined culture. Landon said,

> It was not always that way. As we grew and added branches and divisions, I began to realize that even though our people were very talented, their training just wasn't adequate. After a few months in a new position, especially if they were working in a branch or division location away from headquarters, employees would revert to their old behaviors, what they had learned in school or at their former companies. What was actually happening, of course, was that our rapid growth made it exceedingly difficult to maintain core policies and practices and ensure that employees would avoid the tendencies to take shortcuts and not follow procedures.

As Landon points out, the solution was better communication, which is the main reason why his branch and regional offices today are relatively small, with staffs of between 10 to 20 people. Landon said, "It's much easier to communicate when everyone knows everyone else, and there are no unnecessary layers of management above the supervisors and workers. Organizations with larger numbers of people lose the personal touch and communication. Maintaining a well-defined company culture then becomes difficult at best."

Communication aside, Landon observed that personality types help determine how certain people perform in various roles. Entrepreneurial-minded individuals tend to ignore procedures, be more creative, and act more spontaneously than their corporate-minded counterparts who have a controlling personality. They tend to follow procedures and are less inclined to try out new ideas. The former can be difficult to control, the latter can limit growth, but companies need a mix of each to ensure optimum performance.

Formula for Success

Because companies and their owners are all unique, there is no single formula for success, yet successful entrepreneurs share a few common traits, and one of these is understanding how to treat their most important assets - their employees. Landon takes pride in saying that one of the most rewarding aspects of owning a business is seeing his people grow, especially his long-term employees. He emphasized, "They have become successful and so have I. Honesty, treating people fairly, and being there to help are very important to developing a loyal staff. So, too, is having a genuine interest in their welfare and trying to understand how you would feel in their shoes."

Successful entrepreneurs share another important trait; they have learned how to take on challenges. Landon's approach to solving a problem is to break the process down one step at a time and receive input from people who are living and working with the problem. He said that a common mistake in problem solving is skipping from the problem directly to the solution without addressing the problem's source. "If you fail to identify the root cause of a problem, your solution will likely be a temporary one. So it's important to think the process through and identify all the issues at each step of the way."

Landon identifies the following as the other important keys to his company's success:

- Great market. The Washington/Baltimore market has seen fantastic growth in the corporate and government markets during the last 20 years.
- Strong execution. Perform quality work and develop great relationships.
- Referrals. By building the business through referrals, you ensure that existing clients are completely satisfied with the company's work.
- Differentiation through giving back. Giving back to the community, winning awards both locally and nationally, and becoming active in ALCA (now PLANET) helped created differentiation and a secret weapon in marketing.
- Advertising. Print advertising never took a high priority for Chapel Valley, but Landon now believes that the Internet is going to be the most important future tool in marketing and selling landscape projects.

SURVIVING IN A DIFFICULT ECONOMY

Chapel Valley has been in the mature stage of the business cycle for several years. Management's goal is to continue to manage the business in a healthy manner: to recruit and retain top quality people, produce high quality work, and maintain excellent client relationships. This has been made more difficult thanks to a two-year economic downturn, during which Chapel Valley's sales have decreased by nearly 30 percent.

The financial landscape has changed dramatically for all green-industry companies. The recession has created huge challenges for owners who are trying to be profitable and still maintain quality standards. Being in a recession (this is his fourth) is not a new challenge for Landon. The three previous recessions occurred in 1974, 1981, and 1990. Although the present recession is deeper and broader than its predecessors, Landon is confident that Chapel Valley and the majority of green-industry contractors will survive. His advice for company owners experiencing economic downturns is to take stock of their strengths and focus on the basics. "You have to reduce expenses to match income. This is difficult to do. You'll lose good people and it just isn't fun. Budget cuts will force people and companies to do things differently, run leaner, and keep a closer eye on waste and expenses." Landon says that cutbacks should not be done haphazardly. Owners should take a holistic approach and find a sustainable balance between revenue and expenses. "You have to be aggressive with cost reductions. If you wait too long to make the tough decisions, you will run out of funds and be out of business. The point to remember is that during a long economic downturn success is survival. Those who survive will be in place to reap the benefits when the economy finally turns around."

Landon pointed out, however, that even in a recession opportunities exist. Companies with good resources have great opportunities to position themselves for upturns. Remember, staying in business is the primary objective. Companies with good financial credit and customer relations can do the following:

- Buy out smaller companies.
- Diversify into a different customer base.
- Go green. Develop sustainable environmental, business, and personal models to become more efficient and more productive, all the while differentiating from the competition.

- Look for business niches that complement core business strengths.
- Look for weaknesses in competitors and leverage strengths.

Finally, a recession is the perfect time to work on retaining clients and building stronger business relationships. Take advantage of the fact that many of your customers and potential customers now have time for meetings, which were not possible in the past. Use this time to build relationships and make new contacts.

Down the Road

When Landon first started Chapel Valley, his goals were relatively simple: to become a respected professional in his industry and own and operate a high-quality landscape contracting business. It is obvious that after 41 years, he has achieved these goals in a most impressive manner. He is now turning the business over to his two children: his son, James Reeve, who is company president and CEO, and his daughter, Deonne Wollman, who is vice-president of the construction group and corporate secretary.

At this stage of Landon's career, he sees himself more as a mentor than an actual operating manager. He wants to stay involved in the business but not run it. He is enjoying seeing his son and daughter grow into their respective positions and carry on the family business. Reeve has always believed in continuous learning, as indicated by the numerous conferences and education venues he still attends. This veteran places a high priority on keeping healthy and fit and is focused on his personal wellness. He likes to travel and is taking advantage of this time in his life and career to take trips with his wife and family.

Looking into his crystal ball, Landon sees the economy as the biggest challenge for his company and other green businesses, especially since this recession is so widespread and worldwide. Reeve believes,

"The economy is going to have to get back to level ground and move away from the overgrowth caused by overspending and the excesses that were created in the housing and financial markets." Although Landon is confident that this will happen, it may take awhile to play out.

One of his major concerns is for graduating college students who are suffering as a result of the overspending and excesses of the last decade. They are entering the workforce at a time when entry-level jobs are unavailable and their skills and energies are atrophying due to events beyond their control or responsibility. Landon states, "The economic realities of today are difficult, and new graduates will have to live with them."

Landon sees opportunities in the challenges posed by the economy and the environment. He thinks that the green movement (sustainability) is an exciting new direction for business and those individuals and companies willing to innovate will do well.

Favorite Story

One of Landon's favorite stories took place in the early 1970s when Chapel Valley was a fairly small residential and commercial landscaping company. In the course of operating his business, Landon became familiar with a general contractor who was building a large corporate headquarters, one of the first in the area. For more than three months, Landon had nearly daily contact with the contractor, reviewing plans and presenting ideas. The general contractor liked Landon's ideas so much that he offered the project to Chapel Valley. The landscape estimates exceeded $300,000, which would have been a huge project for the young company. A stumbling block occurred, however, when investors discovered that Landon's company lacked the required bonding, something that was unavailable for such a small operation. Eventually, the general contractor convinced the investors that Landon was trustworthy and presented him as an honest contractor who should be given a chance. The owners agreed, and this project became one of many that helped Chapel Valley become a major landscape player in the area. Looking back Reeve said, "This was a great learning experience. Never give up no matter how daunting the task may be. Believe in yourself, treat people honestly and sincerely, and good things will happen."

DAVE SNODGRASS

Some people know at an early age what they are going to do for the rest of their lives: The Manning brothers and football, John McCain and the military, and John Quincy Adams and government service. For some, it may be an innate calling, for others it may be the influence of a family role model. When both of these factors come together like it did for Dave Sndgrass, it is a recipe for success.

Dave Snodgrass's first business success was in third grade when he took his $0.05 per hour earnings, a total of $0.35, from working in the family business to show and tell. He received such positive feedback from this fellow students and teacher; he knew that this was what he wanted to do for a career. Snodgrass did not necessarily enjoy the chores that earned him his meager salary, but he was proud that he was earning a paycheck and contributing to the family business. Early on he developed an enthusiasm for working with plants that reaffirmed what he wanted to do for the rest of his life. His ambition was to be a businessman, own his own business, and to be independent.

Deep Roots

During the depression years of the late 1920s and early 1930s, Dave's grandfather, who was out of work, started a one-man mowing service. In addition to mowing customers' lawns, Dave's grandfather would prune rhododendrons. His grandmother would take these clippings and propagate them on a three-acre nursery, which evolved into a wholesale business. After Dave's grandfather passed away, his grandmother kept the business alive until Robert Snodgrass married Dave's mother, the daughter, and took over the business.

A Family Affair

As the business grew, so did the Snodgrass family, until there were seven children, all with first names starting with the letter "D": Daryle Lynn, Dennis, Drake, Dan, Dave, Drew, and Dean. Thus, the name "Seven Dees" was born. Everyone in the family worked in the business from the grandmother to the youngest child. This is where Dave learned his work ethic and how to function in a decentralized family structure. It was a great training ground for building interpersonal relationship skills and developing a personal identity.

As a result of mutinies and inabilities to work in harmony, most family businesses fail. When I asked Dave how his multiple-generation family business survived and flourished, he answered that he thinks it is because their father and mother were so busy growing the business, the seven children raised themselves. They sorted out sibling squabbles on their own, split work duties, and learned to work and live together as a family unit. "There is no secret formula or magic, no outside business consultants, nor dictatorial head of family involved." Their experience growing up has served them well in dealing with day-to-day issues. "In businesses when you hire someone from the outside, there is an expectation that the person comes in at entry-level, gains experience, and is promoted according to his or her performance. There is a respect for the hierarchal structure of the organization. This is different in family businesses in which boundaries are not so clear that they create challenges of authority and in which expectations are unrealistic because of senses of entitlements." With the experience of growing up together and developing strong personal bonds and coping mechanisms as a family unit, the Snodgrass family has been able to successfully deal with the problems that plague most large families.

Three siblings remain in the business. Dave is the administrative CEO, Dean is in charge of production and operations, and Drew is responsible for design build and installation sales. Each has his distinct area of responsibility and operates independently within the organization.

Dave consciously avoids the temptation of worrying about whether other family members are carrying their own weights and their shortcomings. He focuses on himself and his personal contributions; he believes that in a family business if you start obsessing on another's lack of performance this is a path to resentment and conflict. To ensure resolution in the case of a major crisis, Dave became the majority owner by buying out his two older brothers.

An observation made by Dave was that the dynamics of working with his brothers was a strong catalyst and motivation for growth. Each brother wanted his area of accountability, and each realized that this could only be possible if they grew the business. This was a strong incentive for everyone to work collaboratively so that ultimately each brother could be successful in his own right.

An Entrepreneur within an Entrepreneurial Organization

Throughout elementary and high school, Dave learned every aspect of the retail and commercial nursery business. When he went to Oregon State University, he was so confident in his technical expertise that he chose to major in marketing with a minor in horticulture. He was confident that he already had all of the agronomic and plant knowledge that he needed and thought to succeed as a business person he would need a strong business and marketing education.

Dave had always worked in his family business, but this did not stop him from following his own dream of owning his own nursery, an entrepreneur within an entrepreneurial organization. Fresh from college, Dave had loans to pay off. His visionary plan for dealing with those loans involved locating and leasing 10 acres of ground, which he rapidly filled with plants. Dave's plan was to grow this business so he could build equity value at the same time that he worked at the family business for hourly wages. In this manner, he thought that he could build a solid foundation to pay off loans and build his career. This was to be Dave's first lesson in the challenges of being an entrepreneur.

After David and his brother Drew finished planting the ground with their nursery stock, the owner of the land informed them that he wanted to break the lease and sell the property. After years of lawsuits and expenses, Dave and Drew prevailed, but it was a Pyrrhic victory and a painful lesson in how challenging running a business can be. Not only did they have to deal with the variables of labor, weather, and market fluctuations but also the unforeseen structural challenges that can blindside and often destroy a business.

PEOPLE AND NUMBERS PERSON

Dave thinks that one of his talents is the ability to bring out the best in other people. He believes people are innately capable and he respects their talents and value. He recommends surrounding yourself with good people who can do things better than you. Even today, he learns new skills from observing others. Dave sees his role as establishing the strategic issues, setting the direction, and allowing his people to do what they do best. Dave also points out that you need to establish high ethical standards so that they permeate the organization. Dave has good analytical skills along with good business instincts. He is proud of his work ethic, which he learned working alongside his grandmother, parents and siblings. He takes satisfaction from others having told him that he has a gift for marketing and business.

MOTIVATION

It is not about the money - it is the sense of accomplishment from creating a business that satisfies clients' wants and needs, helping employees build careers, and building a business legacy that participates and contributes to the community. Dave has pride in building quality products and services. He believes that if all these things are done properly, profits will follow.

Whom Do You Consider to Be Your Greatest Mentor?

Dave credits his father with being his greatest mentor. Dave's father had charisma coupled with strong business acumen. Further mixed in was a strong work ethic that made his father an unbeatable mentor and business role model.

From the beginning Dave knew that he would be successful, the only question was how big that success would be. When his company first reached the million-dollar mark, he was confident that he could grow this number by at least ten-fold. Dave is not bragging nor boasting when he says, "I enjoy my business so much, it is impossible not to succeed." Not a surprising quote from a natural-born businessman.

BURT SPERBER

Many descriptors can be used for Burt Sperber: businessman, entrepreneur, pioneer, innovator, inventor, and family man, but the most apt and one the ones of which he is most proud is horticulturist. Born in 1929 in Los Angeles, just as the iron grip of the Great Depression was taking its toll on businesses in the U.S. economy, Burt's formative years were spent in economic hard times and the harsh reality of World War II. As a young boy, he worked at his father's retail nursery and, as a teenager, for an Italian landscape nurseryman named of Mossimo Giannuli. In 1948, Mr. Giannulli died, and his widow was unable to run the nursery. At the age of 19, Burt and his father purchased the business for $700. Sixty years later the name of the company has changed, but Burt Sperber still comes to work every day as the co-CEO of one of the world's premier, green-industry companies. The name of the company is now ValleyCrest Landscape Companies, with annual sales of $1 billion.

By the 1940s, Southern California was already famous for being the movie capital of the world. In the 1950s, California underwent a population explosion as people were drawn there by the glamour of Hollywood and the lure of almost perfect weather, as viewed during Rose Bowl tournament parades on the recently invented television. With this population explosion, a construction boom occurred in both residential communities and businesses. It was the perfect combination of elements to build a nursery and landscape business: ideal weather, a growing population, and a vibrant economy. Landscape work at the time was an extension of agriculture. The tools, equipment, materials and labor were adapted from farming. Nurseries were primarily small-scale, family operations selling directly to the public. Onto this stage came a teenager named Burt Sperber who, like the hero of a Hollywood script from that era, would live the American dream by going from rags to riches. This "movie" is a blockbuster and there will be no sequels.

Burt's first paying job was working out of his father's nursery. As a preteen, he would help customers seed and fertilize their lawns. He became an expert at hand-seeding lawns and spreading manure, which was used as mulch. He was paid one dollar for approximately 1/2 hour of work, sometimes managing $4 or $5 a day if the jobs were in close proximity. This was big money, compared with the prevailing wage of $0.75 an hour, to a young boy, and it was an important lesson in the value of services. Burt had more spending money than most boys his age. After his father's business failed, Burt worked for Mr. Giannulli, a hard-working, self-taught landscape nurseryman who had been born in Italy and had moved to Los Angeles in the early 20th Century. Mr. Giannulli began to mentor him and soon Burt became a valuable employee. He was a quick learner and this became the foundation for his horticultural training. Mr. Giannulli was schooled in old-world methods of plant propagation, moving trees, and landscape care, which had evolved over centuries. These were also the days of the evolution of irrigation systems. Burt learned the fundamentals of running a landscape nursery and becoming a gardener and soon found that he had a passion for working outdoors and a keen horticultural knowledge for plants. He remembers that he liked the feeling of respect when a customer would ask him to identify a plant.

During the war years and immediately thereafter, money was tight. To help the family finances, Burt would work second and third jobs. These jobs included selling newspaper subscriptions, which proved to be lucrative for someone willing to work hard and sell. Many weeks he was able to bring home an extra $75 in commissions for only 8 to 10 hours of work. Here he learned the importance of relationships in sales, even for commodity items like newspapers. His pitch focused on personal goals: to go to camp, help the family, and go to school. Some of his stories may have been little white lies, but he made the sales and delivered the goods. Burt credits his door-to-door selling experience as the perfect training ground for his success in selling large landscape projects - tell a story and capture their imagination. Even though the money was good, Burt knew that he did not want to make a career being a newspaper salesman. It was not as much fun as physical outdoor labor and working with plants.

As mentioned previously, when Mr. Giannulli died unexpectedly, his widow had no real option other than to offer the business to the young employee. There was not enough money for college, so at the age of 19, Burt asked his father to be an equal partner in the $700 investment to purchase the MG Nursery. His father borrowed money from his father-in-law, and a portion of Burt's share came from his earlier seeding work. With symbolism worthy of a great novel, his seeding savings were invested as seed money into a business that has now grown into a mature cornucopia. American success stories tend to have a simple formula with elements of hard work, intelligence, being in the right spot at the right moment and other readily identifiable intangibles. The formula may be simple, but a rare combination of events must be aligned for there to be lasting success and an indelible mark left on an industry. Like a large river, it is a confluence of many smaller streams with inputs coming from many elements. To successfully make this journey requires a synergy of special skill sets along with timing. Luck may be helpful, but luck is not the deciding factor. A skilled blacksmith named John Deere invented the moldboard plough to tame the Illinois prairies. His innovation became the forerunner of the modern agriculture equipment industry, and the company he founded continues to be a leader. A precocious teenager named Bill Gates dropped out of Harvard and with his partner Paul Allen started Microsoft, which lead the way for the PC revolution. In both these cases, the conditions were ripe for the right persons to come along and change the status quo. These stories are similar to the impact that Burt Sperber and his company ValleyCrest has had on the green industry.

After a few years in partnership with his father, Burt purchased his dad's share and brought in his brother, Stuart, who was eight years younger and had recently graduated from Cal Poly Pomona. Burt gave Stuart a 10% equity stake in the company and made him responsible for running the tree-growing and moving division. During the early years, while Burt was still in his 20s, he recalls that he never considered himself smart. He credits his startup success to being energetic and capable of doing hard physical labor. He prides himself on his endurance, and even today at age 80, he can walk properties with the best estimators. Burt married young and eventually had four children to support. Growing up poor, he had a desire to provide nice things for his family and was willing to do extra work to accomplish this goal. He was also willing to make short-term sacrifices in return for long-term growth and returns. As hard as he worked, Burt soon realized that he was only one person and to build the company that he envisioned, he would have to bring in other people, which he modestly refers to as being smarter than he was. He knew that to hire and retain such people he would have to pay them appropriately. In some cases, that meant paying them more than what he was taking home. On some occasions, when cash flow was tight, he instructed his wife not to cash his paycheck in order to be able to cover payroll. This could happen for several paychecks in a row. They had savings to live on, but it made managing household finances a challenge for his wife, Charlene; they have now been married for 60 years. Later on, this self-denial philosophy paid huge dividends in employee loyalty and retention.

One of the most important factors throughout the history of the company is that customer satisfaction is not just lip service. It is measured by an outside service vendor, and every customer is surveyed. Management rewards are based on customer satisfaction as well as safety, profitability, and employee retention.

In the parlance of a West-Coast surfer, Burt Sperber caught the first wave of the original green movement. This was before the rapid expansion of commercial and residential landscape, before large containerized nursery plants, and before land care services swept the nation. Burt and his colleagues not only saw the big wave coming, they also figuratively invented the surfboard. As I previously described, in the early 1950s, commercial and residential landscape companies and nurseries were primarily operated as stepchildren to big-brother agriculture. Equipment manufacturers were primarily focused on high-volume crops such as fruits and vegetables in California and corn, soybeans, and wheat in the Midwest. Tractors of this era were brutes, designed to haul heavy loads or pull large pieces of equipment. The emphasis was on draw-bar horsepower and not on maneuverability. They were 100% gear and clutch driven, and, in many models, the gears were not synchronized. This was not an efficient combination for doing precision landscape grading on a confined property. Additionally, the accessory implements were limited to front-end loaders and to scraper blades that were either rear or front mounted. A further complication was that many of the tractors had hydraulic and power takeoff systems that worked only when the clutch was engaged. These limitations had major impacts on the productivity and quality of work that could be done on a landscape project.

Frustrated with these restrictions, Burt instructed his mechanics, who were actually kids who liked to work on hot rods, to re-engineer one of his tractors to be hydraulically driven so that with a simple move of a lever it would go as fast in reverse as forward and eliminate the time-consuming task of clutching and switching gears. He also had the scraper blade moved from the front to the rear and had it designed with a curved blade and enclosed sides. This evolved into the omnipresent scraper box. The curved blade with sides was a stroke of genius: the curve and sides allowed dirt to accumulate while the blade leveled high points and the accumulated dirt filled in low spots. It was a gigantic step forward in productivity that revolutionized landscape grading and leveling. Looking at a scraper box today, the design looks simple and even intuitive, but, at the time, building the unit was anything but simple. ValleyCrest had no professional engineers on staff. There was only a non-English-speaking Mexican mechanic who was a wizard with cutting, forming, and welding metal. The final success was accomplished by the tried and true method of trial and error: a real triumph of the Edisonian approach to innovation of "keep trying until you get it right."

For most of us in the green industry, it is hard to imagine a time when there was neither plastic growing containers nor irrigation pipe.

Everything was made out of metal. Earthmoving and grading equipment were borrowed from highway contractors. Backhoes were not mounted on tractors; neither were there skid steers nor small, compact equipment. All that existed were large excavators and large trenchers. The adaptation of two-cycle engines to hand-power tools was yet to be invented. Everything had to be done either by crude brute force or hand labor. It is easy to take for granted all of the modern equipment advances that we now employ, but, 50 years ago, operators filled the void with their own innovations. This creativity did not stop with heavy equipment. Irrigation evolution consisted of developing automatic clocks, the sprinkler heads themselves, electric solenoids for hydraulic valves, and adding motors to mowing equipment. ValleyCrest was the first company to put a motor on a flail mower to mow slopes. Ultimately, many of today's landscape tools came from ValleyCrest inventions and improvements.

Anticipating that "built" landscapes in California would become increasingly popular in both residential and commercial settings and this would create demand for full-grown trees, Burt put his brother Stuart in charge of their tree farm. Up to this point, the majority of nursery trees in the United States were grown in the ground; however, when Burt entered this business, he envisioned an opportunity where others had not. Growing trees traditionally in the ground took a lot of acreage, required a massive amount of labor to dig and burlap for transplanting, and was subject to weather. If it rained, trees could not be dug, and this would hold up landscape jobs. Growing trees in containers is an expensive process, but if transplant losses could be reduced and the propagation cycle made more efficient, this would be a competitive advantage. To start, Burt found that he could get used 15-gallon lard cans from local bakeries. All that was needed to convert a can into a planter was to clean out the residual lard, punch drain holes, fill the can with dirt, and add a plant sapling. When the tree reached a set size, it was either planted at a landscape job or transferred into a larger wooden box. ValleyCrest's tree nursery now encompasses 800 acres.

The brothers' experiences with trees are literally deep-rooted. One of the many skills Burt learned from Mr. Giannulli is the old-world technique for moving a large tree. The procedure is to hand dig around the tree's root ball and encase the ball in a wooden box. Boards are laid under the ball and house jacks are used to lift the tree. Dirt is backfilled into the hole so the tree can be slowly and carefully brought to ground level. The boxed tree is rolled to the street and winched onto a waiting truck. When Burt learned this technique, there were neither front-end loaders nor hydraulic lifts to assist in this task, just manpower and mechanical leverage. Even with the advent of the tree spade, ValleyCrest continues to use this traditional method of tree transplanting. Survival rates are superior, and the health and vigor of the tree are assured; size is limited only by the customer's pocket book.

Even though he was employing a centuries-old method of moving trees from one location to another, Burt did not eschew modern developments to facilitate the job once the tree was dug and on the truck. The next obstacle was placing the tree in its new location. For trees going back into the ground, this was not that great of a challenge, just a reversal of the process used to dig the tree. When, however, the landscape design called for the tree to be placed in a large planter or a confined space, there was no room for all the boards and jacks, and no crane was available that could lift a large tree and its root ball and place these precisely and gently into a confined location. Large hydrolytic lifting arms were not available at the time. The answer to this dilemma was another ingenious solution employing a readily available material - ice. Before mechanical refrigerators became common in every kitchen, food was kept cool in iceboxes, which held large blocks of ice that were delivered weekly from the local ice company and distributor*, so large blocks of ice were readily available,

---

**I fondly remember this extinct business. My grandfather had a thriving coal and ice business in the 1930s and 40s and served as president of the National Coal and Ice Association during this period.*

and the perfect solution emerged: fill the planter with blocks of ice, slide the tree off of the truck, guide it into place so that the root ball was on top of the ice, and let nature take its course. As the ice melted, the tree slowly and gently descended into its new home. The water from the melting ice served to lubricate the sides of the planter and irrigate the root ball.

When the business began its growth phase, Burt realized that if he were to be successful, he had to surround himself with great people. The first year that the company achieved $1 million in sales in the 1950s, it also recorded a 35% profit margin. The CPA's reaction was that this was impossible. The books were double checked and found to be accurate, but this high-water mark was never again achieved - in fact, as the company grew, the profit margin went down. Burt's explanation for this is that when you are personally managing every aspect of the business, you can keep close watch on expenses and maximize production efficiencies; however, this can only happen when the company is relatively small. Once a certain threshold is surpassed, it is impossible for one person to stay on top of everything, and this is where hiring and retaining key employees becomes critical for future success. Hiring workers who share the owner's work ethic as well as his moral values and core values becomes crucial. This is easy to say but difficult to accomplish on a sustainable basis. An equally daunting task is to grow the business while maintaining consistently high operating margins. The reason why some companies fail, some are moderately successful, and others grow to be leaders is the difference in their creativities and abilities to execute. To meet these challenges, it all comes down to the people, and this is where ValleyCrest has excelled and created a human resource powerhouse of training programs and continuing education at all levels of field personnel. In addition to recruiting at various schools, ValleyCrest holds Professors' Summits during which school professors are brought to the Corporate Campus so that the teachers can learn more about the company.

The green industry and especially landscape contracting and maintenance have always been a labor-intensive business and even with equipment advances, labor remains one of the highest costs. Whoever has the most productive and efficient labor force has the ultimate advantage. Burt realized this early on, and this is where he put his focus. All land care operators hire from the same labor pool, have access to the same equipment and material, and in a normal economy (if there is such a thing), can obtain similar lines of credit. The playing field is flat and the barriers to entry are low. The biggest differentiator of companies is the quality of the people hired, trained, and retained. Here again, ValleyCrest was an innovator and brought in an outside consulting firm to assist. ValleyCrest established a sophisticated human-resources department that institutionalized recruiting, training, and performance reviews.

One can have a best-of-class human resources department at corporate headquarters, but if this expertise base is not developed in the various markets where the branches are located, it becomes just another overhead expense. For ValleyCrest, the opposite is true. As an example, in Las Vegas the union hourly labor wage is $55-$65 per hour, so, as Burt puts it, you have to be damned good at scheduling and productivity to maintain profit margins with no waste.

In other non-union markets, the range is $10 to $40 per hour, and he admits it is becoming more difficult to compete because ValleyCrest tends to pay higher wages. To maintain their competitive advantage, improvement teams constantly monitor productivity and issue weekly reports. The union marketplace is a more level playing field when all the companies are paying $55 per hour.

Today, and for the past 60 years, most of ValleyCrest employees are Hispanic, and as a segment they are the highest paid. It is Burt's opinion that Hispanics make the best leaders for their business model. They do this across a multi-cultural employee base of approximately 10,000 people.

Burt observes that being a business owner in today's environment is much riskier than it was just a few years ago. He thinks this is because vendors and manufacturers have ruined the marketplace. By giving credit to companies when the banks will not, profit margins on risky landscape construction work have dropped from 20% profit to 10% profit. Burt thinks the venders should collect on a monthly basis for their product, and their customers should borrow from banks, if necessary, and grow at a healthier speed. Scale is critical, but finding financial backing has become harder. Borrowing money in today's market is almost impossible, and, if you are trying to grow, credit is critical for the purchase of materials and labor. The greater the scale, the greater the capital demands become, and just one large missed receivables payment can spell disaster. ValleyCrest has grown at about 15% annually to become a $1 billion company.

Burt's business philosophy has been to grow the business in a straight line with predictable growth and profits. He has been careful not to grow too fast so good work and efficient crews would be assured and personal client relationships maintained. Employing this approach built a solid reputation for ValleyCrest. When one of their California maintenance and building clients established operations in Florida, ValleyCrest was invited to do the landscape installations and maintenance. From this base, ValleyCrest went on to do the Miami airport and Animal Kingdom in Disney World. This process has been replicated across the country - build good relationships and do good work.

The name ValleyCrest has come full circle. In 1949, when the company first started, it was known as Valley Crest Landscape Nurseries, Inc. Twenty years later in 1969, when stock was offered to the public, the name was changed to Environmental Industries, Inc. Finally in 2002, in an effort to improve brand awareness of the parent company and the various business units, the name was changed back to ValleyCrest Landscape Companies. Presently there are seven business units:

- Design Group - Landscape architects and designers provide specialized services for landscape designs and planning.
- Landscape Development - landscape, hardscape, and sport field installation services from site engineering to construction and design/build

- Landscape Maintenance - commercial landscape renovation, tree care enhancement, and maintenance.
- Golf Course Maintenance - comprehensive course maintenance.
- Residential Design-Build - residential landscape design and installation.
- Tree Company - One of the largest producers of containerized trees in the world and a specialist in large-tree relocation.
- U.S. Lawns - 200 plus franchise landscape maintenance companies located in 32 states.

The combined annual sales are approximately $1 billion with an average total employment of 9,500. The company has a strong presence outside the Continental U.S. with units in Hawaii, Abu Dhabi, the Caribbean, Puerto Rico, and China.

When Burt was asked to name his favorite project, he said that he liked them all, but if he were forced to pick one, it would be the "The Animal Kingdom Park," which was a $75 million project in Disney World. He went on to say that if you have the right budget, you can deliver great results. The bigger the budget, the more spectacular the project will be. There is no secret to selling large jobs - you need a good reputation and need to use every tool at your disposal. One might think that with large projects, clients approach selected vendors, but this is not so. You have to proactively go after the job because the job is not going to come to you. The marketplace is competitive, but with a good track record and fair pricing, you are going to get your share of the large projects.

Sperber did add, however, that one of the advantages ValleyCrest has is its large and reliable tenured workforce. Because the company is so large and diverse with a permanent labor force in place, they can immediately respond to emergencies such as hurricanes and other natural disasters by mobilizing and moving workers across state lines. Even in slow times, the company employs over 9,000. Most other large maintenance companies rely on a temporary work force and, therefore, are not able to mobilize large numbers of employees. This is important to clients who need to be assured that services can be provided during emergencies. Field employees with tenures between 5 and 30 years make up almost 35% of the ValleyCrest's workforce, with 20% having been employed by ValleyCrest for over 10 years. This is incredible considering that ValleyCrest has an average growth of approximately 15% a year. The longevity of its employees allows the company to move quickly as changes in the marketplace occur, and this longevity makes ValleyCrest a great place for employees to have careers and not just jobs.

In terms of second chances, there are not many things Burt would change although he did become animated on the subject of golf course ownership and management. He bluntly put golf in the category of four letter words - GOLF! Although ValleyCrest has a profitable golf course maintenance business, their venture into ownership and management of golf courses fell flat on its face. Bert said that it is one thing to estimate costs to design and build golf courses, but trying to predict demand for courses and providing the types of services that are involved in managing golf courses requires a different business model. He compared it to growing plants versus retailing plants. ValleyCrest is an expert at the former and a novice at the latter.

The daily operations of ValleyCrest were turned over to Burt's son, Richard, in 2000. Under Richard's expert leadership, the company has continued its impressive growth in sales and profitability. The family thinks that the key to success is providing the full spectrum of top-quality horticultural services. The comprehensive integration of these services allows ValleyCrest to be the one-stop source for all the outdoor needs of their clients.

After 60 years as the founder and leader of the company, Burt comes to work every day and relishes his role as historian and mentor. He tries not to intervene in day-to-day operations, but he is available for counsel and particularly gets satisfaction helping others avoid making mistakes that he made. Even though he is now an icon in the green industry and his business accomplishments are legendary, his greatest pride comes from the wellspring of that success - being known as a horticulturist.

DAVE ZERFOSS

In the green industry, Dave Zerfoss's name carries nearly the same awareness as his former employer, Husqvarna. He is an omnipresent leader whose reach spans both fellow equipment manufacturers and greenscape service providers. Dave is a frequent and popular speaker at trade association events. As the former President of Husqvarna Professional Products (U.S.) where he worked for 18 years, he has been an articulate advocate for the benefits of outdoor green living spaces.

Core Values Solid As Granite

Many components go into the formation of one's character. Dave describes this process as a combination of events large and small, starting with a person's earliest memories. For Dave, it was growing up on a small farm in western Pennsylvania with his parents and an older brother, Danny, and learning to appreciate the small things. His father Ernest was one of 13 children. Both Dave's parents grew up in the depression and developed values and religious views that were as solid as Pennsylvania granite. Like many family farms of this period, even though there was a diversity of dairy cattle, hay, fruit, and vegetable crops plus a custom harvesting business, the operation was not self-sufficient. To make ends meet, Dave's father worked multiple jobs and literally burned the candle at both ends. During the day, it was farming and, by evening, factory work. It was a constant drumbeat of getting up early and working late into the night. The only vacation ever taken was on the rare occasion that they could steal a few hours from their daily labors. Taking a well-deserved rest was the closest they ever came to a vacation. A special treat would be a bowl of strawberries enjoyed under a shade tree.

Religion was an important part of the family life. They attended a Presbyterian church that dated to the Revolutionary War and had two of George Washington's bodyguards buried in the cemetery. Dave remembers this as a great environment and a quiet respite from the chores of the farm. Still, he admits that as a young boy sitting through long sermons on a hot Sunday morning was an ordeal. It was a lesson in mental discipline that complemented the physical work of the farm. This was instilled by the firm grip on Dave's hand by his father's strong and calloused hand. It was a force more powerful than the most boring sermon.

Dave fondly remembers his brother Danny, who was five years older, as his first and most influential mentor. Both brothers attended a one-room schoolhouse, and this is where Dave confirmed that his brother was a genius. Dave looked up to and knew his brother was smart, but the teacher's constant comparisons of them convinced Dave of this. As Dave describes it, the family valued academics. Danny helped Dave with his studies, and as a big brother guided him through his adolescent years. Danny's success in academics helped Dave understand that there were opportunities beyond the farm for people who worked and studied hard. A full scholarship to Harvard led Danny to become a renowned professor in medieval history at the University of Delaware.

Dave's formative years were a synthesis of farm, church, and school. Among these, farm work and church attendance were the dominant forces. Elementary and high school were important factors, but what most shaped Dave's character was working alongside his father and brother and participating in church activities. Dave credits the family's custom-harvesting service with introducing him to the art of relationship building. He met interesting people from around the county and worked alongside them as he helped harvest their crops. During strawberry season, not only did Dave pick strawberries, but he also helped load the truck and go to town to sell cartons of strawberries door-to-door, with Dave working one side of the street while his brother worked the other. This is where Dave learned to overcome the fear of a cold call - a talent that paid big dividends in his first paying job after college. Dave allows that you have to knock on a lot of doors to sell a truckload of strawberries!

Participation in church plays and pageants placed Dave in front of an audience. It became apparent that he had a talent for public speaking, and he soon found himself giving presentations at youth conferences. His ability to tailor his talks to audiences' interests, combined with the strength of his faith, allowed him to rise to a leadership position within the church. This accomplishment gave him a new sense of personal identity. Whereas he was always known as Danny's brother when it came to academics, in the church he was known as Dave. Only later did he realize it was a gift to be able to influence people through communications.

Continuous Learning – the Journey Begins

After five years in the one-room schoolhouse, Dave advanced to the "big school" where he was placed in an academic track; however, compared with his brother Danny, he did not feel particularly gifted. Dave's report cards noted that he was persistent and had good skills in this area. On the first day of class in Dave's new school, the teacher asked the class, "What do you want to be when you grow up?" When it was Dave's turn to respond, he had no answer. He said, "I was like a deer in a spotlight." Up to that point, Dave had not thought much about his future, but this question shocked him into thinking there was something wrong with him. He always felt there had to be more to life than working on a farm although he enjoyed living in the country and working alongside his father and neighbors. As a teenager, Dave had no role model other than his brother and his uncles (who worked in factories, drove nice cars, and lived in town). This told Dave that something else was out there; he just was not certain what it was. When Danny went to Harvard, the blinders came off, and Dave realized that there were paths to follow other than the twice-daily walk to the milking barn.

Living 12 miles from school, it was difficult for Dave to participate in extracurricular activities. The family had only one car, and there were endless after school chores. Sports and other teenage rituals of passage were mostly forfeited to church activities. Dave worked hard in high school and knew that he wanted to go on to college, but he also knew that Ivy League scholarships were few and far between.

Where there is a will, there always seems to be a way to make what you want happen. Dave's parents had no money for college, but they could provide room and board in exchange for help on the farm, so Dave enrolled at the local college, Indiana University of Pennsylvania. While at school, he carried a full course load, worked 50 to 60 hours per week, and managed to graduate in four years. He was a liberal arts major with a focus on economics. His studies in finance and economics gave him a solid footing for his career. During this period, not all of Dave's education was taking place in the classroom. One of his part-time jobs was working in a foreign car repair shop where he worked alongside a master technician who taught Dave the art of being a mechanic. This is where Dave learned to break down a system into its components, analyze the situation, make distinctions, and re-assemble the parts to make a better whole. Nothing forces your attention more than tearing down a 12-cylinder Jaguar motor, cleaning each part, repairing and replacing defective pieces, and re-assembling the engine so that it is a smooth-running, high-powered machine. Dave may have been taking liberal arts courses, but his part-time jobs were the laboratories where he began learning the mastery skills needed for a successful business career.

After college, Dave's first job was with Humble Oil and Refining, a part of the company that became Exxon. Here he was exposed to the importance of branding and establishing an identity in the marketplace. In the 1970s and 1980s, there was an abundance of service stations under numerous brand names. Dave's persistence in his job as a sales rep started paying dividends. While his colleagues were more focused on scheduling their next golf games, Dave was working on learning the business and building relationships with operators of the service stations in his territory. Some of the stations were privately owned while others were company operated. This is where Dave learned the work-ethic difference between an owner who had equity in the company and a manager who had no equity or, as they say today, "No skin in the game."

From this position, David advanced to the real-estate division, which was responsible for identifying and purchasing locations for stations and locations for future development. This taught him the importance of strategic planning. Traffic flow, local demographics and future growth projections were all parts of the analysis. Next, Dave was promoted to be a trainer in the human-resources department, and this is where the "professionalization" of his career began.

Before you can educate others, you must become an expert on the subject matter. With Dave's diverse background and his excellent communication skills, he was a natural teacher on a wide range of subjects including technical, mechanical, and high-level business management principles. Exxon was a large company, so the training was world-class, and there were many opportunities available for hard-working, ambitious individuals. Dave was now in his element. He was a sponge for new ideas and soaked up every bit of information that came his way. He listened to every tape that Zig Zigler made, attended countless success seminars, and became so accomplished in teaching professional management that he began giving presentations to independent business groups.

Zerfoss's entry into the green industry began when he was recruited for and accepted the position of a general sales manager for Stihl. His responsibility was to grow the Stihl brand in the handheld tools category. So noteworthy was Dave's success, that Husqvarna offered Dave the presidency of their U.S. division in 1991. Husqvarna prospered mightily under Dave's 18-year tenure and has grown into one of the market leaders in both professional and residential outdoor power equipment.

Dave is a disciple of positive thinking and self-help books. His library is extensive, and he has an encyclopedic memory of what he reads and studies. One of his favorite books is **Outliers: The Story of Success** by Malcolm Gladwell. The book's thesis is that people with equal talents may not all enjoy equal successes. The differentiator is that successful people master their profession by investing over 10,000 hours in their crafts at early ages. This is what separates Venus Williams, Michael Phelps and Bill Gates from others in their professions. Even though each had special talents that were unique to their chosen avocation (physical traits and intellect), they started young and never stop working and striving for improvements. Dave strongly thinks that if people are to master their arts, they have to continually invest in themselves. To reach the top of your profession, you have to have the spirit to want to be a master, and this requires you to balance your skill sets, values, culture and beliefs. There is neither a shortcut nor free pass in this process. As an example of a person who is a master, Dave uses Joe Gibbs. Joe is an accomplished businessman, a NASCAR entrepreneur, and a former NFL head coach. When choosing players to draft for his Washington Redskins football team, Joe talked to the players' junior-high-school coaches and teachers and to others in the communities where the players grew up. He did this to determine if the prospective players had the right character and attitude for success.

"Are You the Best?"

In 2002, at a green industry trade show in Florida, Dave felt a lump on the side of his neck - the lump had not been there the night before. He went home and immediately saw a doctor. After a month of testing, he got the biopsy result: the diagnosis was a full body slam - lymphoma, non-Hodgkin's, T-cell aggressive. The first question that Dave asked his oncologist was, "Are you the best?" When the doctor answered, "Yes," Dave was confident that he was in good hands. The cancer had not spread to his bone marrow, and a combination of chemical and radiation treatments eliminated the cancer. This was an emotional and challenging period in Dave's life. Any work issues became trivial as he focused on his recovery and family relationships. The question, "Am I going to see my grandchildren grow up?" echoed in his mind. A beacon of hope was Lance Armstrong's inspirational book, ***It's Not About the Bike: My***

Journey Back to Life. In his book, Armstrong, who is one of the greatest cyclists of all time, describes his battle back to life after he was diagnosed with advanced metastatic testicular cancer. Part of his battle included winning, multiple times, the world's longest and most challenging bicycle race - the Tour de France. Dave's treatments were successful, and he has now passed the critical five-year mark, which is the standard indicator that a cancer has been cured.

This was another learning experience for Dave. As frightened and concerned as he was during his treatment procedures, he was constantly being exposed to other patients who were sicker than he was. He learned what was important and how to trust and rely on doctors and colleagues. It was a reality jolt in his journey of life and humbling to realize that he was not bulletproof. It was a time of introspection. Dave's core values remained solidly in place and helped him determine who he was, as he was fighting literally for his life. He found that listening and talking to others who were on the same journey brought comfort and perspective to his view of the future. Even though Dave has passed the five-year mark, he maintains his vigil and lives with an awareness that the cancer can recur. He takes strength in knowing that he was able to traverse this portion of his journey of life with the help of others and his own self-reliance. He prefers to view himself not as a survivor but as a victor.

Dave has four children from a previous marriage, two stepchildren from his marriage to his wife Barbara, and six dearly loved grandchildren.

VIEW OF THE FUTURE

Because of its impact on the quality of life of every citizen, Dave thinks the green industry is exceedingly relevant in today's world. Dave pointed out that people have a natural affinity for wanting to be connected to the outdoors. This phenomenon is called biophilia and refers to a person's desire to interact with nature. Focus groups conducted by Husqvarna confirmed that modernization has not stifled this innate desire. This is why people bring plants and pictures of landscapes into their homes and offices. Based upon this, Husqvarna developed the marketing theme "Master Your Great Outdoors." The environmental benefits of green spaces are well documented, and equally important are the psychological benefits that well-maintained outdoor spaces provide. As a result, people will continue to invest in their properties whether they do it themselves or with professional contractors. The opportunity going forward is to find new business opportunities that satisfy these needs. Dave strongly thinks that as an industry we have to be smarter and more aware of global environmental issues.

Defining a Professional

According to Dave, "Professionals are people who do not fit in the middle - they mastered skill sets and invested 10,000 hours to achieve their goals. They want to be the best." In Dave's view, professionals are motivated by monetary rewards and status; however, these are not the primary drivers. The primary drivers are fires to excel at whatever you choose to do. These fires start early in life with the establishment of solid core values and discipline. Dave thinks that there is another important aspect of being a professional that does not get as much focus as it deserves. A complete professional is one who has learned to share both his heart and intellect. This is done even during times when there is not much to share. Paradoxically, it requires a sense of humility to give of oneself to the extent necessary to build a sustainable legacy. From Dave's early farm days to his present position, he has mastered the art of being a humble servant.

EPILOGUE II

There is always a risk of being too philosophical or anecdotal about a person's life and character, but when the final chapter is written and the curtain closes, the eulogy spoken, and the goodbyes are said, it is important to remember this:

It is the playwright, not the play.
It is the worker, not the job.
It is the artist, not the art.
It is the writer, not the book.
It is the founder, not the company.

IT IS THE PROFESSIONAL, NOT THE PROFESSION!

THE FINAL QUESTIONS

- Are you a professional? An entrepreneur? A propreneur?

  ____

- If you are a propreneur:
  In answering the chicken-and-egg causality dilemma, were you first a professional or an entrepreneur?

  ____

  ____

- What is your driver?

  ____

  ____

- What is your future?

  ____

  ____

REFERENCES

Chapter I - Introduction

1. Peter Drucker, ***Management: Tasks, Responsibilities, Practices***, (USA 1973)

Chapter II - Hard Work

1. Lewis Carroll, ***Alice in Wonderland***, (England, 1865)
2. Karl Marx, Capital***, A Critique of Political Economy, Volume 1, Book one: The Process of Production of Capital***, (Germany, 1867)
3. Smith, ***The Wealth of Nations***, (England, 1776)
4. John Keynes, ***The Theory of Employment, Interest, and Money***, (England, 1936)
5. Ayn Rand, ***Atlas Shrugged***, (USA, 1957)
6. Douglas McGregor, ***The Human Side of Enterprise***, (USA, 1960)
7. Tracy Kidder, ***Soul of a New Machine***, (USA, 1981)
8. Malcolm Gladwell, ***Outliers: The Story of Success***, (USA, 2008)

Chapter III - Personal Character

1. George Washington, ***Rules of Civility***, (USA, 1753)
2. Malcolm Gladwell, ***Outliers: The Story of Success***, (USA, 2008)
3. Don Schlitz, ***The Gambler***, (USA, 1978)

4. Michael E. Gerber, ***The EMyth Revisited***, (USA, 1995)
5. Tom Peters, ***In Search of Excellence***, (USA, 1982)

CHAPTER IV - TECHNICAL EXPERTISE

1. The Traveling Wilburys, Traveling Wilburys Volume 3, ***Inside Out***, lyrics by The Traveling Wilburys, (USA, 2007)
2. Rolf Smith, ***The 7 Levels of Change,*** (USA, 1997)
3. Malcolm Gladwell, ***Outliers: The Story of Success***, (USA 2008)

CHAPTER V - SOCIAL SKILLS

1. Doris Kearns Goodwin, ***Team of Rivals***, (USA, 2005)
2. Mac Davis, ***Oh Lord It's Hard to Be Humble***, lyrics by Mac Davis, (USA 1978)
3. Billy Joel, ***The Big Shot***, lyrics by Billy Joel, (USA, 1979)
4. Salt-n-Pepa, ***No One Does It Better Than You***, lyrics by Salt-n-Pepa, (USA, 1993)
5. Carly Simon, ***You're so Vain***, lyrics by Carly Simon, (USA, 1973)
6. Judy Collins, ***Send in the Clowns***, lyrics by Stephen Sondheim, (USA, 1975)
7. Neil Diamond, ***I Am... I Said***, lyrics By Neil Diamond, (USA, 1971)
8. Peggy Lee, ***Is That All There Is?, Lyrics*** by Jerry Leiber and Mike Stroller, (USA, 1971)

CHAPTER VI - PROFILES OF PROFESSIONALS INTERVIEWS

1. Charles Dickens, ***A Christmas Carol***, (England, 1843)
2. Richard Louv, ***Last Child in the Woods***, (USA, 2008)

3. Malcolm Gladwell, ***Outliers: The Story of Success***, (USA 2008)
4. Lance Armstrong, ***It's Not About the Bike: My Journey Back to Life***, (USA, 2001)

About the Author

Bill Hildebolt's appreciation for nature and organic systems started as a boy working on the family farm in Eaton, Ohio. He followed that interest to The Ohio State University where he ultimately earned his Ph.D. in Food Technology. It was at that time that he was introduced to the business world, joining the Campbell Soup Company in their product development group. He rose steadily through the ranks, gaining credit for over 20 patents and ultimately leading the development of Prego Spaghetti Sauce and attaining the title of Vice President.

After spending six years at R.J. Reynolds Tobacco Co., also as a Vice President in the research & development department, Hildebolt decided it was time to get back to nature and to try his hand at entrepreneurship. He founded Nature's Select Premium Turf Services in 1994 with a vision of capitalizing on growing interest in environmental issues by introducing biological lawncare to the market. Even in the competitive world of lawncare, the product was an instant hit with customers. Along the way, though, Bill learned that there was a lot more to being an entrepreneur than just putting out a great product. His insights from over forty years at Campbell Soup, R.J. Reynolds and Nature's Select form the backbone of *The Professional Entrepreneur.*

Currently, Hildebolt serves as Past President for PLANET, the Professional Landcare Network, where he was President from 2009 - 2010. Prior to being elected to the PLANET Board, he served on the Board of Directors for PLCAA, the Professional Land Care Association of America. Throughout his career, he has served on boards supporting his chosen field.

He lives in Winston-Salem, North Carolina with his wife Sandi and son Joe, both of whom have worked at Nature's Select. His two grandchildren, daughter-in-law and another son live in New York. Hildebolt still spends two to three months a year on the family farm back in Eaton overseeing operations and seeking new connections between the land and modern life.